Victorian Ribbon &
Lacecraft Designs

Victorian Ribbon & Lacecraft Designs

Mary Jo Hiney

A Sterling/Chapelle Book
Sterling Publishing Co., Inc. New York

For Chapelle Ltd.

Owners: Terrece Beesley and Jo Packham

Staff: Trice Boerens, Tina Annette Brady, Sheri Lynn Castle, Sandra Durbin Chapman, Holly Fuller, Kristi Glissmeyer, Cherie Hanson, Susan Jorgensen, Margaret Shields Marti, Jackie McCowen, Barbara Milburn, Kathleen R. Montoya, Pamela Randall, Jennifer Roberts, Florence Stacey, Lewis Stoddard, Nancy Whitley, Gloria Zirkel.

Photography: Ryne Hazen

The photographs in this book were taken at Marilyn Mojahed's Victori Ana, Glendale, California; at Anita Louise's Bearlace Cottage in Park City, Utah; and at the homes of Susan Rios, Glendale, California, and Diane Schultz, Glendale, California. Their cooperation and trust is sincerely appreciated.

Library of Congress Cataloging-in Publication Data

Hiney, Mary Jo.
   Victorian ribbon & lacecraft designs / by Mary Jo Hiney.
       p.   cm.
   "A Sterling/Chapelle book."
   Includes index.
   ISBN 0-8069-0402-X
   1. Ribbon work. 2. Lace craft. I. Title. II. Title: Victorian ribbon and lacecraft designs.
TT850.5.H56   1993
746' . 0476--dc20

A Sterling/Chapelle Book

10 9 8 7 6 5 4 3 2 1

First paperback edition published in 1994 by
Sterling Publishing Company, Inc.
387 Park Avenue South, New York, N.Y. 10016
© 1993 by Chapelle Ltd.
Distributed in Canada by Sterling Publishing
% Canadian Manda Group, P.O. Box 920, Station U
Toronto, Ontario, Canada M8Z 5P9
Distributed in Great Britain and Europe by Cassell PLC
Villiers House, 41/47 Strand, London WC2N 5JE, England
Distributed in Australia by Capricorn Link (Australia) Pty Ltd.
P.O. Box 6651, Baulkham Hills, Business Centre, NSW 2153, Australia
Printed and bound in Hong Kong

Sterling ISBN 0-8069-0402-X Trade
            0-8069-0403-8 Paper

Contents

Mary Jo Hiney

Mary Jo remembers embroidering from the age of three while her mother sewed, at a time when sewing was done out of necessity rather than by choice or for recreation and relaxation. She credits her ability now to the influence of her mother, who passed her perfectionism on to Mary Jo.

In fact, Mary Jo attributes her creativity to having mastered the basics as a child seamstress. Today she experiments as she yearned to as a young girl. Ironically, what she has discovered is precision as her taskmaster in her mother's absence. The study of classical piano for eleven years contributed to her exactness and self discipline. Her creations display her work ethic proudly. Discovering that there is life after perfection in work, Mary Jo shares that, "In every other aspect of my life, I have a constant urge to break rules."

After high school, she attended the Fashion Institute of Design and Merchandising in Los Angeles. Later she got her start in the downtown garment industry before moving on to NBC in Burbank, California. Working in the wardrobe department, Mary Jo dressed a diverse group of stars from Lucille Ball to Maureen O'Hara. Eventually the pace in Los Angeles became too restricting, so she and her family moved to the beautiful and tranquil central coast of California. It is here that Mary Jo discovered her creative genius, the love of raising a family and the joy of life. Mary Jo became accomplished in the art of box making while sharing a business with a friend. Her lifelong love of ribbon inspired her to develop many of her own techniques, some displayed in the beautiful works of art found in this book.

The more Mary Jo works with ribbon, the more she unravels the interwoven aspects of her life. It is Mary Jo's hope to inspire others to unleash the "child within" to create their own masterpieces.

To Joshua, Alexis, and Claire
To little Evan and little Mary Jo
To the child within each of us

General Instructions

Before you begin. . .

Cardboard
Heavyweight cardboard is rigid, yet can be cut with scissors, and is used for foundation shapes such as bases, lids and trays. Lightweight cardboard is bendable and is used to mold around foundation shapes.

Clipping Curves/Trimming Corners
Allowances on corners, curves or points should be clipped to create ease and reduce bulk. Clip into allowance at intervals of either ¼" or ½" cutting to, but not through, the stitching.

Glue
When gluing is referred to in projects, use a glue gun and glue sticks to attach embellishments. For boxes, when gluing fabric to cardboard; see *Laminating*.

Marking on Fabric/Ribbon
Mark on fabric/ribbon with an air or water soluble dressmaker's pen. If project cannot be washed, use an air soluble pen. All pens leave a small amount of residue.

Patterns
Supplies:
Dressmaker's pen
Tracing paper

1. Transfer patterns and information to tracing paper. Some patterns are reduced and transferred to a grid to fit on a page. Each square of the grid equals 1".
2. To enlarge patterns, mark grid lines 1" apart on a large sheet of paper. Begin marking dots on 1" grid lines corresponding to the reduced pattern. Connect the dots.

Seam Allowance
Before cutting fabric, add ½" seam allowance to patterns.

Glossary

Beadwork

To attach beads to fabric, bring needle up at 1, through bead and down at 2 (lower left to upper right). Secure, bringing needle up at 3, through bead and down at 4 (lower right to upper left).

Diagram A

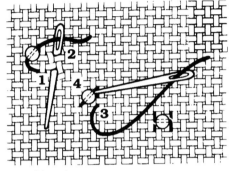

Bud: see Lazy Daisy Leaf/Bud

Bullion Petal Stitch

1. Using one strand of embroidery floss, bring needle up at 1, down at 2, with a loose stitch. Bring needle tip out again at 1; do not pull needle completely through the fabric.

2. Wrap loose stitched floss around needle tip about thirteen times. Holding finger over coiled floss, pull needle through wrapped floss. Insert needle again at 2, pulling to fabric back. If desired, pull floss slightly to curve bullion petal.

3. Stitch petal groups, forming rose as desired.

Diagram B

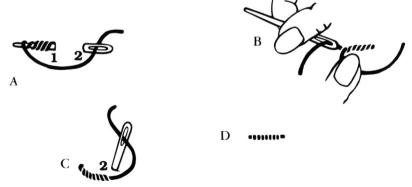

Cascading

Bow Variation: With ribbon length, tie a small bow. Thread needle with tails. *Ribbon Stitch* to fabric very loosely, twisting ribbon between each stitch; place stitches as desired.

Ribbon Length Variation: Repeat, omitting bow.

Diagram C

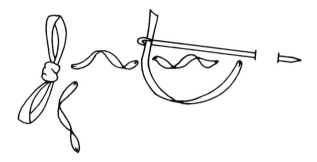

Couching

These stitches are used to anchor a ribbon length to fabric. With embroidery floss or ribbon, bring needle up at 1, down at 2. Repeat to attach ribbon length as desired.

Diagram D

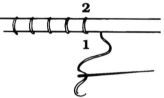

Fabric Leaf/Petal

1. Fold a 2" fabric circle in half, with raw edges aligned. For a crisper leaf/petal, press fabric.
2. With folded edge up, fold into thirds, overlapping sides with raw edges aligned.
3. Stitch running thread on raw edge. Gather tightly. Wrap thread around stitches to secure.

Diagram E

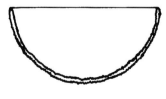 

Ribbon Variation: For ribbon leaf/petal, overlap ends and stitch. Trim excess.

Diagram F

Fabric Petal: see Fabric Leaf/Petal

Fabric Rose

1. Fold fabric strip in half lengthwise with long, raw edges aligned. For a crisper rose, press fabric.
2. Fold fabric ends at right angles. Stitch running thread on long raw edge, leaving needle and thread attached.
3. Gather fabric slightly, simultaneously wrapping to make flower. Force needle through lower fabric edge; secure thread. Trim excess. Fluff.

Diagram G

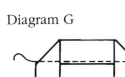 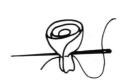

Fabric Yo-Yo

Fold raw edges of a 2½" fabric circle under ¼", stitching running thread on outer edge. Gather tightly. Knot ends to secure. Slightly flatten puckered circle, pressing tightened gathers to center. The smooth side is bottom and gathered side top.

Diagram H

Fern Stitch

Using ribbon length, work from top to bottom of frond, bringing needle up at 1, down at 2. Bring needle up at 3, down again at 1. Bring needle up at 4, down again at 1. Repeat, until desired length is achieved.

Diagram I

Fluting

Fluting is usually used as a border. Attach one ribbon end to fabric, loop to desired length, and glue. Repeat making a series of even loops.

Diagram J

French Knot

Using one strand of embroidery floss or ribbon length, bring needle up at 1. Wrap floss/ribbon around needle two times. Insert needle a short distance from 1, pulling floss/ribbon until it fits snugly around needle. Pull needle through to back.

Diagram K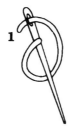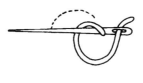

Gathered Circle

1. Fold ribbon in half with right sides facing and edges alligned. Stitch ends.
2. Sew running thread on one long edge. Gather tightly; secure thread. Flatten.

Knife Pleating

Pin ribbon pleats ½" deep and ½" apart, all in same direction. Press. Stitch on one long edge to secure.

Diagram L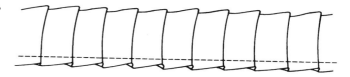

Laminating

Supplies:
Paper (to cover work surface)
3" disposable paint roller
Paint tray
Tacky glue (thin bodied)

1. Pour glue in paint tray. (It is important to keep hands free of glue while laminating; a damp rag may be useful.)
2. Place cardboard on covered work surface. Saturate paint roller with glue, rolling on paint tray to remove excess. Roll a thin coat of glue on surface of cardboard as indicated in directions.
3. Place cardboard, glue side down on wrong side of fabric. Turn, smoothing fabric over cardboard with hand. Glue raw edges to back. Shape laminated cardboard while still pliable and before it is completely dry.

Lazy Daisy Stitched Leaf/Bud

Using one strand of embroidery floss for leaf and ribbon length for bud, bring needle up at 1, down at 2, with a loose stitch. Bring needle up on one side of floss/ribbon at 3, then back through fabric on opposite side at 4. A bud is often finished at 1 and 2 by a French knot.

Diagram M

Mitering

To miter, fold and/or stitch edges at a 45° angle. Trim excess as indicated.

Diagram N

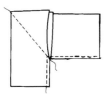

Ribbon Stitch

Using ribbon length, bring needle up at 1, down at 2, repeat as desired.

Diagram O

Pencil Daisy

1. Holding two pencils 1" apart, loop ribbon length back-and-forth, over-and-under, alternating pencils.
2. Loosely stitch running thread between pencils. Gather tightly. Wrap thread around stitches and knot to secure.
3. Remove pencils, fluff and separate petal loops.

Diagram P

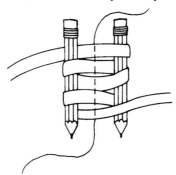

Ribbon Leaf

1. Fold ribbon length in half lengthwise, with long, wired edges aligned. Turn folded ribbon corners up to within ⅛" from wired edge.
2. Stitch running thread. Gather; secure ends. Open and shape leaf.

Diagram Q

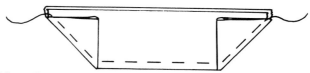

Ribbon Loops

1. With a dressmaker's pen, mark ½" allowance on each end of ribbon. Measure and mark loop length from first mark as shown, adjusting for length and number of loops as indicated in directions with ⅜" between each loop.
2. Beginning at one end, fold ribbon, aligning 1 to 2. Stitch running thread through aligned marks. Gather tightly. Wrap thread around stitches to secure. Repeat with remaining marks to form additional loops.

Knotted Variation: Mark ribbon as above, then mark center of each loop. Knot ribbon loosely at center marks. Tie all knots first, then stitch as above.

Diagram R

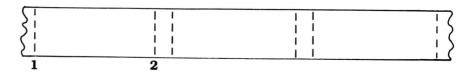

Ribbon Rosette

1. For ⅛" rosette, cut 5" ribbon length; for ¼" rosette, cut 9" length. Mark center of ribbon length. Beginning at one end, fold end forward at right angle. Holding vertical length, begin rolling ribbon at fold horizontally to form bud.

2. Then, fold horizontal ribbon backward at right angle and continue rolling bud, aligning top edges of bud to second fold (rounding corner).

3. Continue folding ribbon backward at right angles and rolling bud to center mark. Secure, leaving needle and thread attached.

4. Stitch running thread on edge of remaining ribbon length. Gather tightly. Wrap gathered ribbon around bud. Secure and fluff flower.

Layered Variation: Layer lengths of ribbon. Handling as one, fold and stitch as above.

Diagram S

   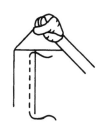

Ribbon Weaving

1. Tape edges of muslin to work surface with double-sided tape. Beginning ½" from bottom edge, place ribbon strips side-by-side horizontally on muslin. Attach both ends of each strip to double-sided tape. Secure ends only with masking tape. Repeat vertically, attaching one end of each remaining strip to double-sided tape. Cover attached ends only with masking tape.

2. With blunt needle, weave ribbons one at a time. Tape remaining edge with masking tape. Lift woven piece, covering back of double-sided tape with masking tape.

Diagram T

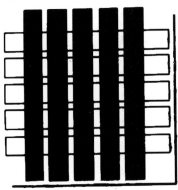 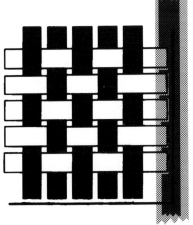

Ruching

1. With a dressmaker's pen, mark ½" allowance on each end of ribbon. Measure and mark at intervals from first mark as shown, adjusting for length as indicated in directions.

2. Stitch running thread on first interval marks. Gather tightly; secure. Cut thread. Repeat on remaining interval marks, gathering ribbon length.

Layered Variation: Layer two ribbon lengths. Handling as one, mark and stitch as above.

Diagram U

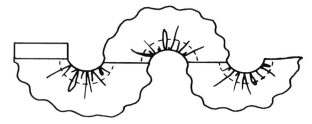

Running Thread

Using thread, bring needle in and out of fabric in loose ¼" intervals, leaving long tails for gathering. If preferred, where appropriate, machine stitch.

Satin Stitch

Using ribbon length, bring needle up at 1, down at 2, making loose, parallel stitches to fill pattern. Keep ribbon flat, stitching closely and evenly beside adjacent stitches.

Diagram V

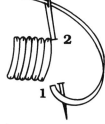

Scallops: see Violet

Scoring

Supplies:
Ruler/straight edge
Utility knife
Pencil

1. Score cardboard, according to directions; dotted lines on patterns indicate scoring.

2. With ruler as a guide, lightly cut halfway through cardboard with utility knife. The cardboard will bend easily with the cut side out.

Slipstitch
With a needle and thread, make small, almost invisible stitches. Slipstitching is used to secure a folded edge to a flat surface.

Diagram W

Tack
To tack fabric or trim is to join two or more layers with small, inconspicuous hand stitches.

Violet/Scallops
1. With dressmaker's pen, mark ½" allowance on each end of ribbon. Measure and mark scallop length from first mark, adjusting for length and number of scallops as indicated in directions. Unless otherwise indicated, violet petals always measure 1⅝".
2. Stitch running thread as indicated. Gather tightly.
3. For flower, stitch short ends, forming a circle. Wrap thread around stitches to secure. Trim excess ribbon below stitches; fluff.

Diagram X

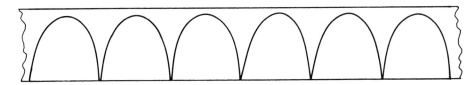

Whipstitch
Whipstitch is usually used to join two finished edges, but it can also be used to secure an edge to a background fabric. Using a single strand of thread (unless otherwise indicated) knotted at one end, insert needle at 1, pick up a few threads of both layers of fabric, bringing it out at 2.

Diagram Y

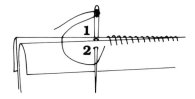

Cherished Trinket Keeper

MATERIALS

4" x 22" pink moire
6" x 9" white satin
6" x 9" fleece piece
12" of ⅝" white scalloped lace
3" white lace fabric
⅛" silk ribbon:
    ½ yard of blue
    ⅜ yard of green
    ⅜ yard of light green
    10" of burgundy
    10" of tan
    10" of yellow

⅜ yard" of 1" mauve ribbon
⅝ yard of ⅜" mauve ribbon
10" of ¼" dark pink ribbon
9" of ¼" white silk ribbon
¼ yard of ½" dark pink silk ribbon
¼ yard of ¼" white trim
Green silk embroidery floss
Three assorted brass charms
20 assorted pearls and pink seed beads
3" x 15" heavyweight cardboard piece
2¼" x 8" lightweight cardboard piece
½" x 6" dowel

DIRECTIONS

1. Make patterns. Cut cardboard, fabric and fleece, according to chart.

	HEAVY WT.	LIGHT WT.	PINK	WHITE	FLEECE
	CARDBOARD				
LID TOP	1		adding ½"		1
LID CENTER	1		adding ½"		1
INSIDE LID	1			adding ½"	
LINING SUPPORT		½" x 6⅜"		6" circle	
BOX SIDE		2" x 7⅝"	3" x 9"		
BOX BOTTOM	1				
BASE	1		adding ½"		

2. Glue fleece to LID TOP. Center cardboard/fleece LID TOP, fleece-side down, on wrong side of pink LID TOP. Pulling snugly, wrap and glue edges to wrong side. Repeat, layering lace fabric over LID TOP. Repeat for INSIDE LID, omitting lace.

3. Center and laminate BASE and LID CENTER. Laminate BOX SIDE, centering cardboard on wrong side of pink BOX SIDE. Pulling snugly, wrap and glue one short end and two long edges to wrong side, clipping corners. Let dry slightly.

4. To shape, lay BOX SIDE right-side down. Place dowel at one short end. Roll cardboard tightly around dowel. Place BOX SIDE around BOX BOTTOM. Begin gluing outer edges of BOX BOTTOM to inner edge of BOX SIDE, small sections at a time. Complete, overlapping short ends and gluing finished end on top. Glue ¼" ribbon over seam, folding raw edges under BOX BOTTOM and inside box.

5. For hinges, cut two 1½" lengths of ¼" dark pink satin ribbon, set remaining ribbon aside. Glue one end of one length ½" from seam on inside top edge of box; hang free end outside box. Repeat with remaining length on opposite side of seam. Pad inside of box bottom with batting scrap.

6. Finger gather lining, gluing wrong side to LINING SUPPORT. Fold lining (right-side in) through center, covering cardboard sides. Beginning at seam, align top edges, gluing LINING SUPPORT flush with top edge of box. (Leave hinge ends free outside seam.) Glue ¼" white trim on inside top edge, covering seam.

7. Glue scalloped lace on wrong side of BOX BOTTOM edge. Center and glue wrong sides of BASE and BOX BOTTOM together. Glue 1" ribbon around bottom of box. Form two loops at seam.

8. Place INSIDE LID right-side down on box opening. Glue free ends of ribbon hinges to back. Center and glue right side of LID CENTER and wrong side of INSIDE LID together. From remaining ¼" dark pink satin ribbon, tie a small bow. Knot tails. Glue inside box at seam between hinges.

9. To embellish LID TOP, make twelve ⅛" rosettes: two each of burgundy, gray, peach, pink, tan, and yellow ribbon. Make one ¼" rosette from white ribbon. Make one ½" violet from dark pink ribbon. Trace heart on LID TOP. Arrange and glue ribbon embellishments on heart outline. With ⅛" green ribbon, stitch leaves around rosettes. With embroidery floss, stitch leaves as desired. Cascade ⅛" blue silk ribbon around rosettes. Attach pearls and seed beads at random. Glue one charm under rosettes and two charms at center.

10. Flute ⅜" mauve ribbon on wrong side of LID TOP edge. Center and glue wrong sides of LID TOP and LID CENTER together.

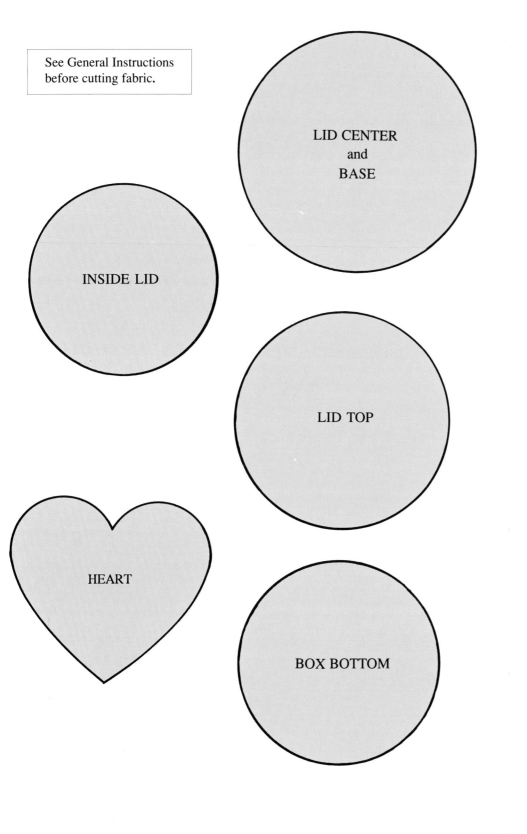

See General Instructions before cutting fabric.

LID CENTER
and
BASE

INSIDE LID

LID TOP

HEART

BOX BOTTOM

Birthday Remembrances

MATERIALS

⅝ yard of cream satin
⅜ yard of white satin
8" x 10" fleece piece
1½" x 15" peach strip
¾ yard of 1½" flat cream scalloped lace
¾ yard of ½" cream trim
2 yards of ⅜" tan organdy ribbon
2 yards of ⅜" white organdy ribbon
Assorted lace scraps
⅛" silk ribbon:
    1 yard of yellow
    ½ yard of pink
    ½ yard of green
    ½ yard of mauve

¼" silk ribbon:
    1¾ yards of yellow
    1½ yards of pink
    ¾ yard of gold
6" of ½" pink wired ribbon
100 each of burgundy and silver seed beads
Four small cream buttons
One small brass button
One 3" tan tassel
Batting
Purchased, old-fashioned greeting card
15" x 32" of heavyweight cardboard
1" x 6" dowel
Masking tape

DIRECTIONS

1. Cut cardboard, fabric and fleece, according to chart. Score cardboard pieces as indicated (see Diagrams A and B on page 28).

	HEAVY WT. CARDBOARD	WHITE	CREAM	FLEECE
BOX	10⅛" x 12⅛"		4½" x 24"	
BOX COVER	7" x 13"	8½" x 14½"	2 (1½" x 6¾")	
OUTER BINDING	3" x 7"		4½" x 8½"	2¾" x 6¾"
INNER BINDING	2¾" x 6⅝"		4½" x 8½"	
FRAME	5" x 7"		6½" x 8½"	4¾" x 6¾"
BASE	5" x 7"		6½" x 8½"	
BOX LINING		10" x 12"		

2. For window, center and mark greeting card outline on cardboard FRAME. Mark ¼" inside outline. Following inside outline, cut window in FRAME. Cut fleece to match FRAME.

3. Glue fleece to cardboard FRAME. Center cardboard/fleece FRAME, fleece-side down, on wrong side of cream FRAME. Pulling snugly, wrap and glue edges to wrong side. Cut window in cream FRAME, leaving ½" on window edges. Clipping corners, wrap and glue edges to back. Repeat with OUTER BINDING, omitting window opening.

4. Center and laminate INNER BINDING and BASE. On BOX COVER, glue one 1½" x 6¾" cream strip over scores. Turn to unscored side. Laminate BOX COVER, centering cardboard on wrong side of white BOX COVER. Pulling snugly, wrap and glue edges to scored side, clipping corners. Let dry slightly. Fold on scores. Roll dowel across folds, making distinct corners.

5. Fold cardboard BOX on score lines. Tape corners. Laminate outside of cardboard BOX, gluing long edges of cream BOX around inside of BOX. Glue remaining long edge to bottom of BOX, clipping corners. Place batting inside BOX.

6. Align and glue long edge of BOX LINING, ⅛" below one top inside edge of BOX, box pleating corner. Repeat, gluing each side and pleating corners. Repeat until all sides are attached. Glue ½" trim flush around top inside edge of BOX LINING, covering raw edges.

7. Flute tan organdy ribbon around two short and one long bottom outside edges of BOX and each short end of INNER BINDING. Repeat with white organdy ribbon on wrong side of all BASE edges and short ends of OUTER BINDING.

8. Arrange and glue lace scraps around greeting card edges as desired. Set aside. Mark ½" intervals around FRAME window. Cut one 36" length each of ¼" yellow and pink ribbon. Handling as one, begin at one corner of window and couch ribbon at each interval, twisting ribbon loosely between each stitch. Stitch five seed beads over couching at each interval.

9. Make one fabric rose from peach strip and one ¼" layered ribbon rose with yellow and gold silk ribbons. Make three petals from pink wired ribbon. Glue to FRAME front at top left corner as desired. Cut one 18" length of yellow ⅛" ribbon. Tie a small bow. Attach under peach rose. Cascade tails, loosely crisscrossing at top edge of FRAME front. Secure cream buttons over crisscrosses.

10. Center right side of greeting card in FRAME window, taping to wrong side of FRAME. On wrong side of FRAME, glue straight edge of scalloped lace to edges, pleating at corners to fit. Tack lace over each corner on FRAME front.

11. Center and glue wrong side of FRAME to one 5" x 7" side of BOX COVER (scored-side out). Repeat, gluing wrong side of BASE to remaining 5" x 7" side of

BOX COVER. Center and glue OUTER BINDING to BOX COVER on outside edge between FRAME and BASE; see photo. Center and glue INNER BINDING to BOX COVER on inside binding. Center unfluted BOX side on INNER BINDING inside BOX COVER. Glue BOX bottom to BOX COVER and BOX side to INNER BINDING.

12. Handling remaining ⅛" and ¼" ribbons as one, tie bow. Glue to center outside edge of FRAME front. Knot tails. Glue gold button and tassel to center of bow.

Diagram A

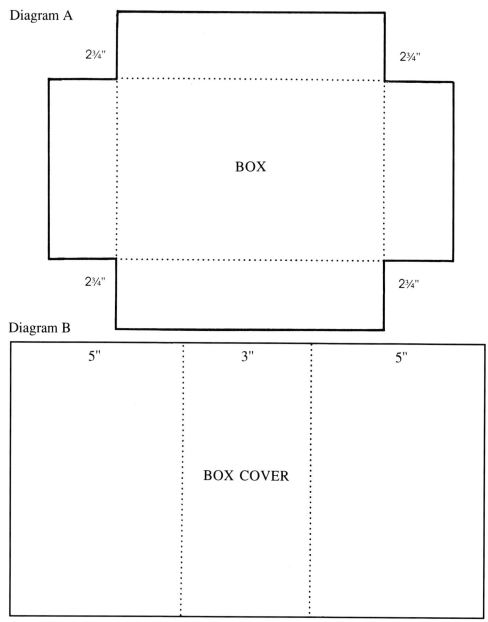

Diagram B

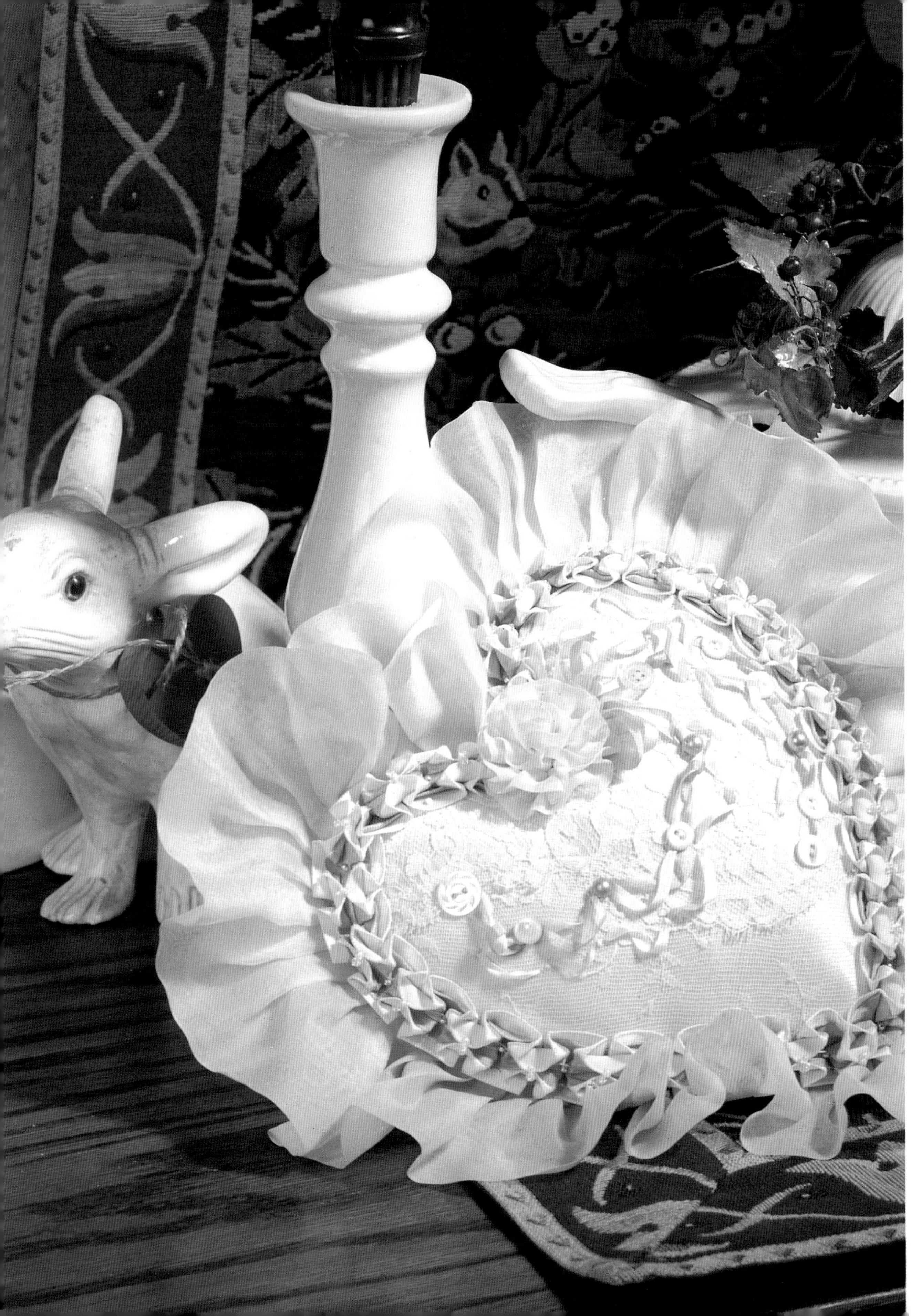

Ruffled Rhapsody

Ruffled Rhapsody

MATERIALS

8" x 16" cream satin
8" cream lace square
½ yard cream silk organza
⅛" silk ribbon:
    1¼ yards of tan
    ⅝ yard of cream
    ⅝ yard of peach

1¾ yards of ½" gray wired ribbon
1¾ yards of ⅞" cream satin ribbon
100-125 seed beads
Nine assorted small cream buttons
Three large pearls
Polyester stuffing

DIRECTIONS
All seams are ¼".

1. Make pattern. Cut two hearts from satin. Cut one heart from lace to cover heart front. Layer one satin heart and lace, right sides up; pin and stitch edges together.

2. To make ruffle, cut two 5" x 35" strips of organza; set remaining aside. Stitch short ends together. Fold with long edges aligned; press. Stitch knife pleats ⁵⁄₁₆" apart. Press pleats 1" from raw edges. Stitch running thread on one long edge. Gather. Pin ruffle to heart front, right sides facing; stitch. With right sides facing, stitch front to back, leaving a 2" opening. Clip seam allowance at cleavage; turn. Stuff firmly and slipstitch opening closed.

3. Center and glue ½" gray ribbon over ⅞" cream ribbon. Make ½" box pleats along length of ribbons (see diagram). Stitch center to secure pleats. Cut 22" of ⅛" tan ribbon; set remaining ribbon aside. Glue tan ribbon on pleat seam. Center and stitch one seed bead between each pleat. Pinch and glue centers of each box pleat; see diagram and photo. Stitch three seed beads to center of each pinched pleat.

4. Pin pleated ribbon to edge of pillow; trim to fit. Finish raw edges. Beginning at center front, hand stitch in place.

5. Cut 1½" x 8" strip from remaining organza. Make a fabric rose. Attach at cleavage. Handling all remaining ⅛" ribbon as one, tie a small bow. Attach at right side of rose. Cascade tails. Stitch beads, buttons and pearls, as desired.

See General Instructions
before cutting fabric.

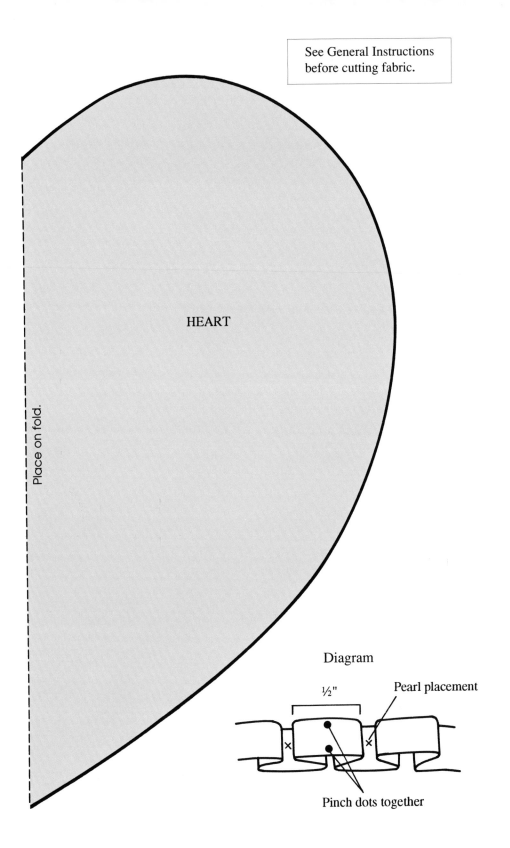

HEART

Place on fold.

Diagram

½"

Pearl placement

Pinch dots together

Heartfelt Memories

MATERIALS

6" x 21" taupe moire
6" x 6" brown lining
5" fleece square
⅛" silk ribbon:
    1 yard of pink
    ¾ yard of mauve
    ¾ yard of tan
    5" of lavender
    5" of purple
    5" of taupe

½" wired ribbon:
    ¼ yard of lavender
    ¼ yard of mauve
    ¼ yard of purple
1 yard of ⅜" tan organdy ribbon
11" of 1" brown wired ribbon
11" of tan braid
½ yard of gold metallic braid
Silk embroidery floss: cream, green, pink
Fifteen assorted pearls and seed beads
10" x 12" lightweight cardboard piece

DIRECTIONS

1. Make patterns. Cut two frames, two backs and two stands from cardboard. From taupe fabric, cut two frames, one back and one stand. From brown fabric, cut one back. From fleece, cut one frame.

2. Glue fleece to one cardboard frame. Clip edges of one taupe frame. Center cardboard/fleece frame, fleece-side down, on wrong side of taupe frame. Pulling snugly, wrap and glue edges to wrong side. Repeat with remaining cardboard and taupe frame, omitting fleece. Flute and glue organdy ribbon to outer edge on wrong side of one taupe frame. Center and glue wrong sides of frames together. Glue tan braid to inner edge of frame on seam.

3. Make five ⅛" rosettes: one each from lavender, mauve, pink, purple and taupe ribbon. Make three violets from ½" lavender, mauve and purple wired ribbon. Glue one pearl to center of each violet.

4. To embellish front, cut one 5" length of 1" brown ribbon. Tie small bow. Attach to upper left of heart. Glue violets below bow. Glue rosettes spaced at ¼" intervals on right half of heart. From remaining ⅛" pink ribbon, stitch buds; place as desired. From remaining ⅛" mauve and tan, stitch ferns and leaves around buds. From floss, scatter bullion petals and leaves around buds. Attach remaining beads and pearls as desired.

5. Clip edges of taupe back. Center one cardboard back on wrong side of taupe back. Wrap and glue edges to wrong side. Repeat with remaining cardboard back and brown back. Cut slash marks through taupe back, according to pattern. Set aside.

6. Center cardboard stand on wrong side of taupe stand. Wrap and glue sides and wide end to wrong side of cardboard, leaving top edge extended; set aside. Trim remaining cardboard stand slightly, cutting slash mark. Insert one end of remaining brown ribbon ½" through slash; glue. Center and glue wrong side of stands together. Insert free end of ribbon and extended edge of taupe stand through corresponding slashes on taupe back; glue. Center and glue wrong sides of backs together. Glue metallic braid to outer edge of back on seam. Center and glue bottom three-fourths of taupe frame back to brown side of back, leaving top open to insert photograph.

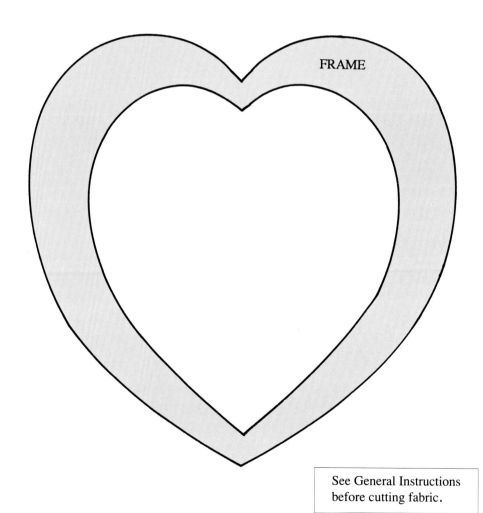

FRAME

See General Instructions
before cutting fabric.

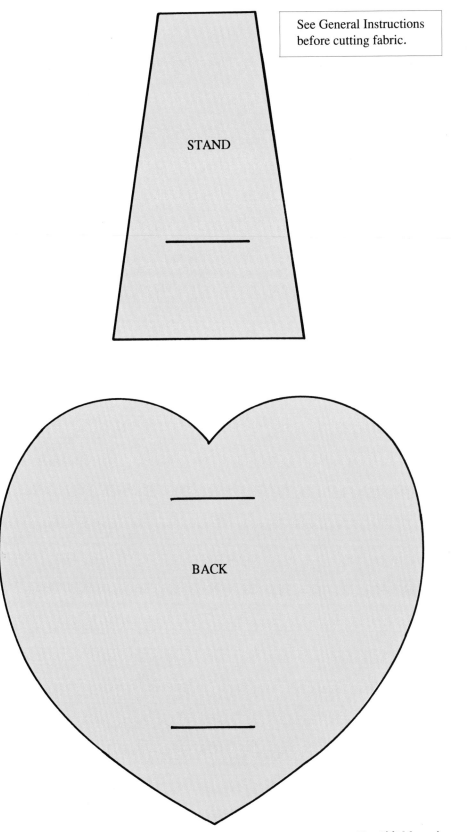

STAND

See General Instructions before cutting fabric.

BACK

Sew, Sew Intriguing

MATERIALS

Fourteen 6" x 12" coordinating prints
One 2¾" x 18" coordinating strip
8" fleece square
5" gold metallic lace square
⅛" silk ribbon:
    ½ yard of brown
    ½ yard of cream
    ½ yard of pink
    ½ yard of tan
    ½ yard of yellow

⅝ yard of ¼" gold metallic flat trim
⅝ yard of 1" brown wired ribbon
¼ yard of 1½" brown ribbon
¼ yard of 1¼" green velvet ribbon
Eleven assorted buttons
One brass charm

5" x 15" heavyweight cardboard piece
20" x 30" lightweight cardboard piece

DIRECTIONS

Note: To make a box with two coordinating fabrics, substitute ½ yard of print fabric for outside and ½ yard coordinating fabric for inside in place of fourteen coordinating fabrics.

1. To make BASE, cut the following—
    From heavyweight cardboard:
        One 4¼" square
    From coordinating prints:
        One 5¼" square
Center and laminate BASE to wrong side of fabric. Pulling snugly, wrap and glue edges to back, clipping corners.

2. To make LARGE PANEL, cut the following—
    From lightweight cardboard:
        One LARGE PANEL, according to pattern
    From coordinating prints:
        Five 5" x 6" pieces
Score LARGE PANEL; see pattern. With scored side down, laminate panel center with one fabric piece, trimming excess fabric from corners. With scored side up, center and laminate each panel with one 5" x 6" fabric piece. Pulling snugly, wrap and glue edges to wrong side. Trim excess fabric from corners, leaving panel center uncovered. Turn. Allow to dry slightly, folding LARGE PANEL on scores.

3. To make LARGE LINERs, cut the following—
    From lightweight cardboard:
        Four 3⅞" x 4⅞" pieces

From coordinating prints:

    Four 4⅞" x 5⅞" pieces

    Four 4⅞ " x 5" pieces

    Two 4⅞" x 3¼" pieces

Center and laminate each LARGE LINER to wrong side of one 4⅞" x 5⅞" fabric piece. Pulling snugly, wrap and glue edges to wrong side, clipping corners. For each large pocket, fold one 4⅞" edge of each 4⅞" x 5" piece under ½". Place one folded edge 1" from one short edge of LARGE LINER. Pulling snugly, wrap and glue side and bottom edges to wrong side. Repeat for remaining large pockets. Repeat with remaining 4⅞" x 3¼" pieces for small pockets, placing 1" from large pocket tops. Center and glue wrong sides of each LARGE LINER to each LARGE PANEL.

4. To make SMALL PANEL, cut the following—

    From lightweight cardboard:

        One SMALL PANEL, according to pattern

    From coordinating prints:

        Five 3½" x 4½" pieces

Follow Step 2 for SMALL PANEL.

5. To make SMALL LINERs, cut the following—

    From lightweight cardboard:

        Four 1⅜" x 2⅜" pieces

    From coordinating prints:

        Four 2⅜" x 3⅜" pieces

        Four 2⅜" x 3" pieces

        One 6" circle

Follow Step 3 for SMALL LINERs and large pockets. Stitch running thread around circle. Gather slightly, stuffing center. Gather tightly, forming pin cushion. Glue gathered edges to small panel center.

6. To make LID, cut the following—

    From heavyweight cardboard:

        Two 4¼" squares for LID TOP/INSIDE LID

    From lightweight cardboard:

        One ¾" x 16¾" LID SIDE

    From coordinating prints:

        Two 6" squares

    From fleece:

        Four 4" squares

Layer and glue fleece to one LID TOP. Center cardboard/fleece LID TOP, fleece-side down, on wrong side of one print square. Pulling snugly, wrap and glue edges to wrong side, clipping corners. Repeat with remaining INSIDE LID and fabric.

Laminate LID SIDE and 2¾" x 18" strip, centering LID SIDE horizontally and leaving ½" allowance on one long edge of strip. Pulling snugly, wrap and glue one short end of strip to wrong side. Glue long edge, aligning raw edges. Let pieces dry slightly. Fold on scores, making corners. Place LID SIDE (seam allowance down) around INSIDE LID (right-side up), aligning corners (see diagram). Beginning at first corner, glue outer edge of INSIDE LID to inner edge of LID SIDE. Continue gluing small sections at a time. Complete, overlapping short ends, gluing finished end on top. Glue allowance to wrong side of INSIDE LID. Center and glue wrong sides of LIDs together.

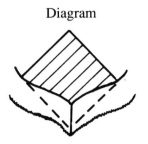

Diagram

7. Center and glue SMALL PANEL center over LARGE PANEL center on the diagonal. Center and glue wrong sides of BASE to LARGE PANEL bottom. Glue one LARGE PANEL to one inside edge of LID.

8. Center and glue metallic lace over LID. Pulling snugly, glue to LID SIDEs. Beginning at center back, glue metallic trim around LID SIDEs, covering lace edges. With 1½" brown ribbon, tie bow. Attach to center of LID. Handling ⅛" ribbon lengths as one, tie bow. Attach to center of brown bow. Knot tails. Make two ribbon leaves from velvet. Attach leaves to bows. Glue three buttons and one charm to LID as desired.

9. At 2" intervals, cinch and glue 1" brown wired ribbon around lip of BASE. Glue remaining buttons on each cinch.

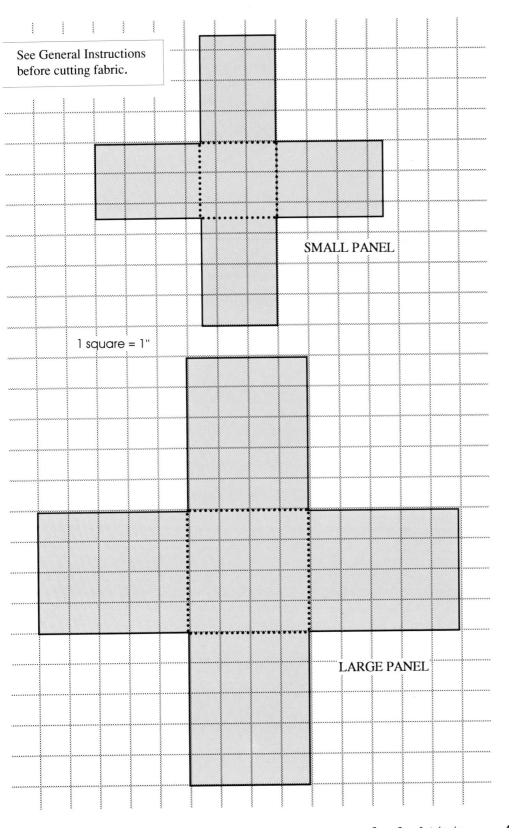

See General Instructions
before cutting fabric.

SMALL PANEL

1 square = 1"

LARGE PANEL

Treasures of the Heart

MATERIALS

½ yard of yellow print
½ yard of coordinating yellow print
½ yard of fleece
¾ yard of 1" white lace
1½ yards of small gold metallic braid
⅛" silk ribbon:
    ½ yard of blue
    ½ yard of purple
    ½ yard of yellow

¼ yard of ¼" green satin picot ribbon
1 yard of 1" green satin wired ribbon
5" of 3" tan lace
Eleven assorted plastic and metal buttons
Batting
1" x 6" dowel
28" x 44" heavyweight cardboard piece
7" x 27" lightweight cardboard piece

DIRECTIONS

1. Make patterns. Cut cardboard, fabric and fleece, according to chart. Score lightweight cardboard pieces in half parallel to short ends.

	HEAVY WT. CARDBOARD	LIGHT WT. CARDBOARD	PRINT	COORDI-NATING	FLEECE
LID	2		adding ½"	adding ½"	2
LID SIDE		1" x 26⅜"	3" x 27½"		
TRAY	2			adding ½"	
TRAY SIDE		1" x 25"		3" x 26½"	
INSERT BOTTOM	1			adding ½"	1
INSERT SIDE		2" X 25¼"		3½" x 26½"	2" x 25¼"
BOX SIDE		3½" x 25⅝"	6" x 26"		
BASE	1		adding ½"		
SEAM BINDING			2½" x 7"		

2. Glue and layer fleece pieces to one LID. Center cardboard/fleece LID, fleece-side down, on wrong side of print LID. Pulling snugly, wrap and glue edges to wrong side. Repeat with INSERT and INSERT SIDE, gluing fleece on unscored INSERT SIDE.

3. Center and laminate remaining LID, TRAYs, and BASE.

4. Laminate BOX SIDE on scored side, centering cardboard on wrong side of print BOX SIDE horizontally, leaving ¼" allowance on one long edge and 2" on opposite long edge. Pulling snugly, wrap and glue edges to wrong side, clipping corners.

5. Laminate LID SIDE, centering cardboard horizontally, leaving ½" allowance on one long edge and 2½" on opposite long edge. Pulling snugly, wrap and glue one short end to wrong side. Glue long edge to cardboard, aligning raw edges. Set aside. Repeat with TRAY SIDE. Let side pieces dry slightly.

6. To curve, lay BOX SIDE right-side down. Fold score, rolling dowel across fold making a distinct corner. Unfold, turning right side up. Place dowel on short end, rolling cardboard around dowel to center score. Repeat on opposite end. Repeat to curve LID SIDE and TRAY SIDE. Repeat for INSERT SIDE, beginning with padded-side up.

7. Place TRAY SIDE (seam allowance down), around one coordinating print TRAY (right-side up), aligning corners (see diagram). Beginning at first corner, glue outer edges of TRAY to inner edge of TRAY SIDE. Continue gluing small sections at a time. Complete, overlapping short ends and gluing finished end on top. Glue allowance to wrong side of TRAY. To form handles, cut two 4½"

Diagram

lengths of picot trimmed ribbon. Glue short ends together. Glue ends to wrong side of TRAY, one on each side, 5½" from cleavage. Center and glue wrong sides of TRAYs together. Repeat to complete LID and INSERT, omitting handles.

8. Fold SEAM BINDING into thirds lengthwise. Glue right side of SEAM BINDING to wrong, upper edge of cleavage on INSERT. Repeat Step 7, gluing BOX SIDE around INSERT. Cover seam with SEAM BINDING. Center and glue wrong sides of BASE and INSERT together.

9. Cut two 27" lengths of gold metallic braid. Glue one braid length along outside edges of LID seam. Repeat with remaining length on box bottom along edges of BASE. Glue 1" lace to BOX SIDE just above braid.

10. To embellish lid, cut lace scrap to fit upper left curve of LID; glue. Knot ends of 1" green ribbon. Tacking with glue, loosely flute border halfway up left side and across top edge of LID. Handling three ⅛" silk ribbons as one, tie a small bow. Glue bow to upper left curve. Cascade tails. Glue buttons randomly around ribbons.

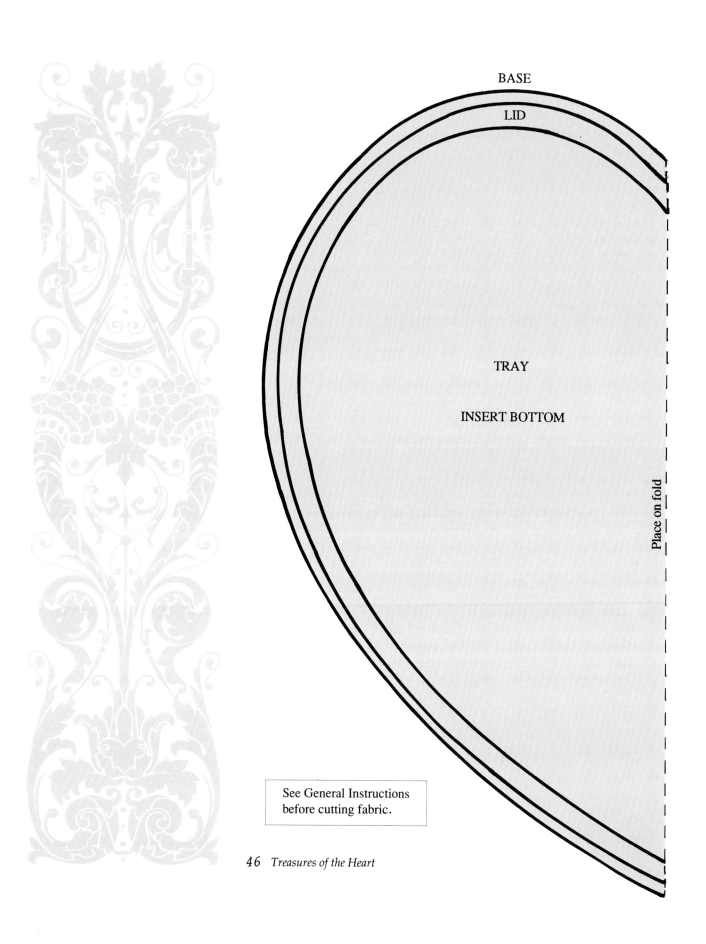

BASE

LID

TRAY

INSERT BOTTOM

Place on fold

See General Instructions
before cutting fabric.

Heart of Gold

MATERIALS

3" x 6" cream fabric
1½" x 6" gold fabric
1½" x 15" cream chiffon
1¼" x 15" yellow fabric
3" fleece square
5" of 1" metallic wired ribbon
⅛" silk ribbon:
    ½ yard of light gold
    ½ yard of dark gold

¼" silk ribbon:
    ¼ yard of light yellow
    ¼ yard of dark yellow
5" of ½" flat cream lace
½ yard of gold metallic braid
5" of cream/gold metallic picot trim
10-12 assorted small buttons and pearls
4-6 brass charms
3" lightweight cardboard square

DIRECTIONS

1. Make heart pattern. Cut one heart front and one back from cardboard. From cream fabric, cut one heart front and one heart back. From fleece cut one heart.

2. For front, glue fleece to cardboard front. Clip edges of fabric hearts. Center cardboard/fleece front, fleece-side down, on wrong side of fabric front. Pulling snugly, wrap and glue edges to wrong side. For back, glue remaining cardboard back to fabric back.

3. From gold braid cut one 6" length half; set remaining aside. Fold length in half, tying a knot 1" from folded end. Glue tails to wrong side of heart back.

4. Make a fabric bow from 1½" x 6" strip of gold fabric. Make a fabric flower from 1¼" x 15" strip of cream chiffon. Make two loops from 5" of 1" wired ribbon. Make two ¼" rosettes: one each from light yellow and dark yellow ribbon. Make four ⅛" rosettes: two each from light gold and dark gold ribbon.

5. Glue fabric bow to knot on hanger. Glue loops to fabric bow at angle. Glue one charm on fabric bow, opposite loops. Center fabric rose and glue to fabric bow; see photo.

6. Embellish heart front with charms and rosettes as desired. Cut one 12" length each of ⅛" light and dark gold ribbon. Handling as one, tie a small bow. Attach to cleavage of heart front. Cascade tails on either side. Glue buttons and pearls to cascaded tails. Loosely wrap picot trim to heart front, gluing ends to wrong side.

7. For ruffle, press 1¼" x 15" strip of yellow fabric, matching long edges. Stitch running thread along raw edges. Gather to fit heart. Beginning at top of cleavage, glue ruffle to wrong side of heart front three-quarters around. Glue cream lace around remaining quarter of heart.

8. Center and glue wrong sides of heart front and back together. Wrap and glue remaining gold braid around seam of heart back.

HEART

See General Instructions
before cutting fabric.

DIAMOND
for *All That Glitters*
on page 56

Stitch in Time

MATERIALS

9" x 11" peach fabric
8" x 10" fleece piece
Assorted lace and doily scraps
⅛" silk ribbon:
    ¾ yard of cream
    ¾ yard of mauve
    ½ yard of tan
    ½ yard of yellow

Two ¼ yard lengths of pink ¼" silk ribbon
Silk embroidery floss: light green, pink, tan
75-100 assorted beads, brass charms, pearls,
    sequins
Five small cream buttons
8" x 10" pre-cut mat
8" x 10" lightweight cardboard piece
8" x 8" heavyweight cardboard piece
Masking tape

DIRECTIONS

1. Cut fleece to cover mat front. Repeat with peach fabric, adding 1" seam allowance to all edges and clipping inside corners.

2. Glue fleece to mat board front. Center front, fleece side down, on wrong side of peach fabric. Fold edges to back and glue. Hand stitch collage of lace and doily scraps to front.

3. Make four ⅛" rosettes, one each from cream, mauve, tan and yellow ribbon. Glue to mat front. Tie a small bow from one 17" length of ⅛" cream ribbon. Attach to top left corner of window. Cascade tails. Repeat with one 9" length of ¼" pink ribbon. Attach to bottom center of window. With remaining ⅛" tan and yellow ribbon, make small bows, placing as desired. With remaining ⅛" mauve ribbon, stitch buds at random.

4. Embellish front with beads, charms, pearls, sequins and buttons, following designs in lace. Embroider bullion roses and leaves with floss as desired. Place photo in window; secure with tape. Center and glue wrong sides of mat front and back together.

Vision of Love

MATERIALS

5½" x 11" dusty rose moire
5½" dusty rose satin square
¼ yard of white lining
Thirteen 2½" assorted fabric circles
5" x 9" fleece piece
⅜ yard of ¼" white picot trim
⅛" silk ribbon:
  ¾ yard of pink
  ½ yard of dusty rose
  ½ yard of green
  ½ yard of light green
  ⅜ yard of gold
  15" of burgundy

10" of mauve
10" of tan
10" of yellow
7" of purple
6" of 1" brown wired ribbon
3" of ¼" pink satin ribbon
Embroidery floss:
  Three pink shades
  Two green shades
Assorted pearls and seed beads
Batting
4½" x 20" heavyweight cardboard piece
3" x 11" lightweight cardboard piece

DIRECTIONS

1. Make heart patterns on page 103. Cut cardboard, fabrics and fleece (F), according to chart. Score lightweight cardboard piece as indicated (see Diagram A).

	HEAVY WT. CARDBOARD	LIGHT WT. CARDBOARD	ROSE SATIN	MOIRE	WHITE LINING	F
LID TOP	1		adding ½"			1
LID CENTER	1			adding ½"		1
INSIDE LID	1				adding ½"	
LINING SUPPORT		½" x 9⅞"				
BOX BOTTOM	1					
BOX SIDE		2½" x 10⅞"		4" x 12¼"		
BASE	1			adding ½"		
LINING					adding 2½" to inside bottom	

2. Glue fleece to LID TOP. Center cardboard/fleece LID TOP, fleece-side down, on wrong side of satin LID TOP. Pulling snugly, wrap and glue edges to wrong side. Repeat with INSIDE LID.

3. Center and laminate BASE and LID CENTER.

4. Laminate BOX SIDE on scored side, centering cardboard on wrong side of moire BOX SIDE. Pulling snugly, wrap and glue one short end and two long edges to wrong side, clipping corners. Let dry slightly.

5. To curve, lay BOX SIDE right-side down. Fold on score. Roll dowel across fold, making distinct point. Unfold. Place dowel at one short end on wrong side of cardboard. Roll cardboard tightly around dowel to point. Repeat on opposite short end.

6. Place BOX SIDE around BOX BOTTOM, aligning point. Beginning at point, glue outer edges of BOX BOTTOM to inner edge of BOX SIDE. Continue gluing small sections at a time. Complete, overlapping short ends, gluing finished end on top.

7. For hinges, cut 3" length of ¼" satin ribbon in half. Glue end of one length 1" from cleavage on inside top edge of box; hang free edge of ribbon outside box. Repeat with other piece on opposite side of cleavage. Place small amount of batting inside box.

8. Finger gather lining, gluing wrong side to LINING SUPPORT. Fold lining (right-side in) through center, covering cardboard sides. Beginning at point, align top edges, gluing LINING SUPPORT flush with box edge. (Leave free hinge ends outside seam.)

9. Center and glue wrong sides of BASE and BOX BOTTOM together. Make a small bow from 1" brown wired ribbon. Attach bow to cleavage at lip of BASE. Make thirteen yo-yos from fabric circles. Beginning at point, glue yo-yos along lip of BASE.

10. Place INSIDE LID right-side down on box opening. Glue free edges of ribbon hinges to back. Center and glue right side of LID CENTER and wrong side of INSIDE LID together. Cut one 7" length of ⅛" pink ribbon; set remaining aside. Handling 7" lengths of ⅛" pink and purple ribbons as one, tie a small bow. Knot tails. Glue bow inside box at cleavage between hinges.

11. To embellish LID TOP, make nine ⅛" ribbon rosettes: three of burgundy ribbon and two each of mauve, tan and yellow ribbon. Attach to LID TOP as desired. With ⅛" green, light green and gold ribbon, stitch ferns and leaves around rosettes. With remaining ⅛" pink ribbon, stitch buds as desired. With floss, embroider bullion petals and leaves around buds. Attach pearls and seed beads at random.

12. Weave ⅛" dusty rose ribbon through picot trim. Glue trim on wrong side of LID TOP edge. Center and glue wrong sides of LID TOP and LID CENTER.

All That Glitters

MATERIALS

2½" x 5" brown fabric
3" fleece square
⅛" silk ribbon:
    10" of beige
    10" of brown
    10" of burgundy
    10" of gold
    10" of mauve
    10" of olive
    10" of teal

¼ yard of ½" green wired ribbon
¼ yard of 1" brown wired ribbon
¼ yard of ⅛" burgundy picot trim
4" of ⅜" gold metallic trim
10-15 Assorted large beads, metal
    buttons, pearls, rhinestones
1" pin back
1½" x 3" lightweight cardboard piece

DIRECTIONS

1. Make diamond pattern on page 49. Cut two diamonds each from cardboard and brown fabric. From fleece, cut one diamond.

2. For brooch front, glue fleece to one cardboard diamond, clipping edges. Center cardboard/fleece front, fleece-side down, on wrong side of fabric front. Pulling snugly, wrap and glue edges to wrong side. Repeat with remaining cardboard and brown diamond for brooch back, omitting fleece.

3. Make fourteen ⅛" rosettes: two each of beige, brown, burgundy, gold, mauve, olive and teal. Embellish pin front, gluing beads, buttons, pearls, rhinestones and rosettes as desired. Loop picot trim around embellishments, securing ends to cardboard back.

4. Make one ribbon leaf with ½" green wired ribbon. Center and glue wrong side of brooch front over ribbon leaf; see photo. Make one ribbon leaf with 1" brown wired ribbon; set aside.

5. Cut two 2" lengths of metallic trim. Center each length on top and bottom points of brooch front; glue to wrong side. Center and glue wrong side over brooch front to brown ribbon leaf.

6. Center and glue wrong sides of brooch front and back together. Glue pin back to brooch back.

Elegant Chapeau

MATERIALS

Purchased straw hat
1 yard of 18" cream scalloped
   embroidered netting
¾ yard 1½" cream jacquard ribbon
¾ yard 1½" tan wired ribbon

5½" cream lace doily
15-18 straw flowers
Six assorted large buttons
Rhinestone pin

DIRECTIONS

1. With scalloped edge up, stitch cream netting around hat crown, draping width loosely on brim. Tack doily, off center, to side of crown and brim at hat front. Attach four buttons and pin as desired near doily. Pinch brim at center front; stitch.

2. Make violet, marking six 4" scallops on tan wired ribbon. To form center, wrap first scallop tightly and remaining scallops loosely. Following rosette instructions, make one bud from one 8" length of jacquard ribbon. With remaining jacquard length, make two loops, leaving one 6" tail.

3. Attach loops to center hat back, allowing tail to hang over brim. Stitch ribbon and straw flowers to right of looped bow. Stitch remaining buttons to left of looped bow on side of crown.

Fashionable Accent

MATERIALS

1 yard of 1½" pink wired ribbon
1¼ yards of 2" sheer pink ribbon
1½" pin back

DIRECTIONS

1. Cut one 25" and one 11" length from 1½" wired ribbon. Tie a four-looped bow with 25" length; clip tails. Tie two-looped bow with 11" length; clip tails. Center and glue to four-looped bow.

2. Make ribbon rose from 2" sheer ribbon. Glue to center of bow. Glue pin to back.

Variation

Charming Little Cherub

MATERIALS

3" x 6" light green moire
3" fleece square
⅛" silk ribbon:
    ½ yard of green
    ½ yard of ivory
    ½ yard of pink
    6" of coral
    5" of burgundy
    5" of gold
    5" of light pink
    5" of mauve
    5" of peach
    5" of purple
    5" of tan
    5" of yellow

7" of ⅝" gathered cream lace
5" of 2" cream lace
6" of ½" sheer metallic organdy ribbon
¼" silk ribbon:
    ½ yard of pink
½" silk ribbon:
    1⅝ yard of pink
    1⅝ yard of yellow
4" of ¼" cream picot trim
Three brass charms
Three small flat cream buttons
Embroidery floss: dark pink, blue
3" x 6" lightweight cardboard piece

DIRECTIONS

1. Make cherub face pattern. Cut one face front and one back from cardboard. From green fabric, cut one face front and one back. From fleece, cut one face front.

2. Glue fleece to cardboard front. Clip edges of green faces. Center cardboard/fleece front, fleece-side down, on wrong side of green front. Pulling snugly, wrap and glue edges to wrong side. For back, glue cardboard back to green back.

3. With dark pink floss, straight stitch eyelashes; see pattern. With blue floss, lazy daisy stitch eye. Cut 10" of ¼" pink ribbon. Stitch a running thread on one long edge. Gather. Repeat with remaining 8" piece. Set aside.

4. Make twenty-eight 2" layered ribbon petals with ½" pink and yellow ribbon. Beginning on back of face front, glue one row of eleven petals on edge of head. On face front, glue a second row of nine petals ¼" from first row. Glue a third row of six petals ¼" from second row. Glue remaining two petals at center of face ¼" from third row. Glue 10" ruffled ribbon between first and second row of petals. Repeat with 8" ruffled ribbon between second and third row of petals. Glue two charms behind third row. Glue three buttons behind two-petal row; see photo.

5. Make eight ⅛" rosettes: one each from burgundy, gold, light pink, mauve, peach, purple, tan and yellow ribbon. Glue on last row of petals. Weave ⅛" coral ribbon through picot trim. Glue in front of rosettes; secure ends to back of face front.

6. Beginning at neck back and ending at nose, glue gathered lace to edge of wrong side of face front. Stitch a running thread on one long edge of organdy ribbon; gather. Glue to edge of face front from forehead to neck front. Gather 2" lace and glue under neckline to back of face front. Fold 2" ribbon length in half for hanger. Glue ends to top back of face front.

7. Center and glue wrong sides of face front and back together. Handling ½" lengths of ⅛" green, ivory and pink ribbons as one, tie small bow. Attach to neck. Knot tails. Glue remaining charm to center of bow.

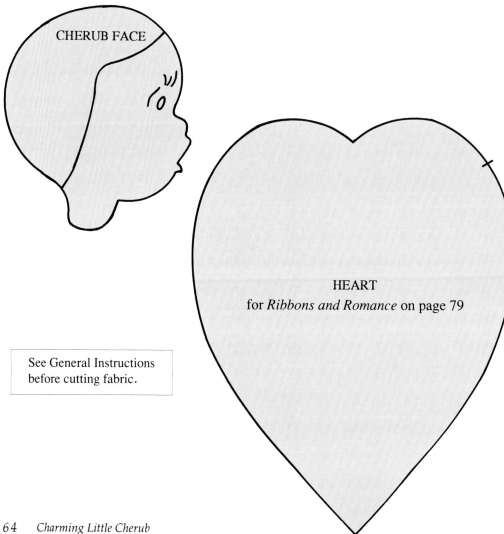

CHERUB FACE

HEART
for *Ribbons and Romance* on page 79

See General Instructions before cutting fabric.

Sugarplum Fairy

MATERIALS

8" green fabric square
8" pink fabric square
1 yard of 4½" purple wired ribbon
¾ yard of 1" green wired ribbon
1½" wired ribbon:
    2¾ yards of printed metallic
    1⅜ yards of fuchsia

½" wired ribbon:
    15" of purple
    ¼ yard of fuchsia
¾ yard of ¼" green silk ribbon
1½ yards of ⅜" fuchsia organdy ribbon
One green iridescent button
¾" high porcelain doll head with shoulder plate
7" x 14" lightweight cardboard piece

DIRECTIONS

1. Make pattern. Cut two cones from cardboard and one each from green and pink fabric.

2. Center and glue wrong side of green fabric to one cardboard cone. Repeat with pink fabric on remaining cone. Carefully roll green cone with fabric right side out and pink cone with fabric right side in. Overlap straight edge of each cone; glue.

3. Stitch running thread on one long edge of green wired ribbon. Gather to fit wide end of green cone; glue inside wide end, overlapping ribbon ends. Place green cone over pink cone, sandwiching ruffle between cones. Align seams opposite each other; glue together.

4. For cone ruffles, gather one long edge of 27" length of printed ribbon. Stitch ends. Gather to fit green cone, ⅝" from wide end; glue. Repeat with one 24" and one 21" length of printed and one 18" length of 1½" fuchsia ribbon; glue to cone in tiers ⅝" apart.

5. For skirt, fold 4½" purple ribbon ends at a 90° angle. Stitch running thread diagonally across angle and around top edge; trim ends (see diagram). Gather tightly, securing ½" from top of cone. Shape to form skirt.

6. Glue doll head to flattened cone top, facing ribbon opening. Press firmly and allow to dry. For bodice, cut one 28" length of 1½" fuchsia ribbon. Mark seven 4" scallops. Sew running stitch on scallops. Gather tightly, forming small and large scallops. Glue small scallops to bottom of shoulder plate with large scallops down, overlapping ribbon ends.

7. Cut one 5" length of ½" purple ribbon. Tie a bow. Attach to center front scallop. Glue button to center of bow. For wings, tie a four-looped bow from one 24" length of printed ribbon, trimming tails. Shape and glue to center back scallop.

8. Make three layered ¼" rosettes, each with one green ribbon and two organdy ribbons. Glue one rosette to scallop on each shoulder. Set remaining rosette aside. Make a gathered circle from one 9" length of ½" fuchsia ribbon. Glue to top of doll head. Repeat with ½" purple ribbon. Attach to center of fuchsia circle. Glue remaining layered rosette to center of purple circle.

Diagram

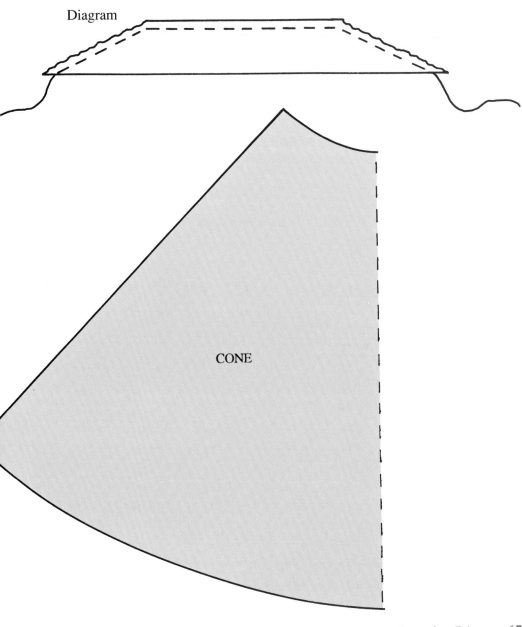

CONE

Heartwarming Teapot

MATERIALS

6" x 10" cream satin
6" x 5" cream tulle
6" x 5" fleece piece
⅛" silk ribbon:
    1 yard of coral
    1 yard of burgundy
    ½ yard of dusty rose
    ½ yard of light green
    ½ yard of olive green
    ¼ yard of gold

¼" silk ribbon:
    1¼ yards of cream
    ½ yard of gold
    ¼ yard of dusty rose
    ¼ yard of tan
⅝ yard of cream/gold metallic picot trim
⅝ yard of gold metallic braid
Green silk embroidery floss
Twelve pink seed beads
6" x 9" lightweight cardboard piece

DIRECTIONS

1. Make teapot pattern. Cut one teapot front and one back from cardboard. From cream satin, cut one teapot front and one back, omitting handle. From tulle, cut out one front, omitting handle. From fleece cut one front, omitting handle and spout.

2. Glue fleece to cardboard front. Clip edges of satin teapots. Center cardboard/fleece front, fleece-side down, on wrong side of satin front. Pulling snugly, wrap and glue edges to wrong side. Repeat, layering tulle front over satin front. For back, glue remaining cardboard back to satin back.

3. Cut ¼" cream ribbon in half, wrapping and gluing to each handle. From picot trim, cut one of each length: 6½" for handle, 4 ½" for bottom, 3½" for lid and 2½" for spout, attaching as desired; see photo. Fold remaining 5½" length in half. Tie a knot 1" from fold. Glue raw ends to wrong side of one teapot lid.

4. Tie small bow from one 12" length of coral ribbon. Glue to teapot lid, cascading tails. Make two ¼" layered rosettes: one with ⅛" burgundy, ¼" gold and dusty rose ribbons; one with ⅛" coral, ¼" gold and tan ribbons. Make five ⅛" rosettes: one coral, three burgundy and one dusty rose. Glue one rosette to center of coral bow on teapot lid. Attach remaining flowers as desired.

5. With remaining ribbons, stitch buds and leaves. Embroider bullion petals and leaves as desired with floss. Attach beads at random. Center and glue wrong sides of teapot front and back together. Glue gold braid to teapot edges.

TEAPOT

See General Instructions
before cutting fabric.

SMALL CONE
for *Nostalgic Nosegay* on page 77

70   *Heartwarming Teapot*

Woven 'Fan'tasies

MATERIALS

5" x 12" print fabric
5" x 6" fleece piece
5" x 6" gold metallic tulle
3½" muslin square
3" fusible webbing square
½ yard of ¼" pink picot trim
¼" silk ribbon:
   9" of pink
   9" of yellow
   3" of green
⅝ yard of ⅜" pink organdy ribbon
7" of ⅝" green wired ribbon to
   cover handle

⅛" silk ribbon:
   2 yards of pink
   1⅝ yard of green
   1⅝ yard of purple
   1⅝ yard of tan
   1⅝ yard of light yellow
   ⅝ yard of bright green
   10" of peach
   10" of medium yellow
   10" of dark yellow
Green silk embroidery floss
Two brass fan charms
Assorted pearls
5" x 12" lightweight cardboard piece

DIRECTIONS

1. Make patterns. Cut one fan front and one back from cardboard. From print fabric, cut one fan front and one back, omitting handle. From tulle, cut one front, omitting handle. From fleece, cut one front, omitting handle.

2. Glue fleece to cardboard front. Clip edges of print fans. Center cardboard/fleece front, fleece-side down, on wrong side of print front. Pulling snugly, wrap and glue edges to wrong side. Repeat, layering tulle front over print front. For back, glue cardboard back to print back.

3. For woven ribbon heart, cut 27" lengths each of ⅛" pink, green, purple, tan and light yellow ribbons. Cut each length into six 4½" strips. Weave. Trace and topstitch heart on bias on right side of ribbons. Repeat, stitching 1/16" outside of first row. Fuse webbing to back, according to manufacturer's instructions. Cut heart 1/16" outside stitching. Center and fuse heart to fan front.

4. Make fifteen ⅛" rosettes: two peach, three pink, two purple, two tan, two light yellow, two medium yellow and two dark yellow ribbon. Glue on woven heart edge, to within ¾" of point on either side. Glue charms to heart on either side of point; see photo.

5. Cut ⅝" lengths each of ⅛" green, pink, purple, tan and light yellow ribbons;

add organdy ribbon length. Handling as one, tie a small bow. Glue to point. Cascade ⅛" pink ribbon tails on fan front. Knot remaining ribbon tails. Make one ¼" layered rosette with pink and yellow ribbons, gluing to center of bow. Make two ¼" green ribbon petals, gluing on either side of rosette.

6. With 18" lengths each of ⅛" green and bright green silk ribbon, stitch leaves around rosettes and cascaded tails. Glue pearls on cascaded tails.

7. Center and glue wrong sides of fan front and back together. Wrap and glue green wired ribbon around handle. With remaining 2" ribbon length, make hanger, gluing to center back of fan.

FAN

HEART

See General Instructions before cutting fabric.

Romantic Interlude

MATERIALS

Purchased pink silk camisole
⅛" silk ribbon:
   2¼ yards of white
   1½ yards of pink
   ¾ yard of cream

½ yard of 3" flat white lace
¾ yard of ⅜" gathered cream lace
Eight rice-shaped cream beads
One package of iridescent seed beads
Eleven small flat cream buttons

DIRECTIONS

All seams are ¼".

1. With right sides facing, align white lace ends at underarms and long straight edge with neckline. Miter lace at center front fold; stitch and trim. With right side up, slipstitch in place, folding under raw edges. Beginning at top edge of one side seam, slipstitch ⅜" cream lace to underarms and neckline, folding under raw edges.

2. Stitch first button to center front of camisole over cream lace. Stitch remaining buttons at 1" intervals along neckline.

3. Cut one 9" length of ⅛" white ribbon. Tie small bow. Attach ½" below center button. Make nine ⅛" rosettes from white ribbon; set remaining ribbon aside. Following rosette instructions, make five buds, using a 3" length of pink ribbon for each. Stitch flowers as desired.

4. Loosely stitch white, pink and cream ribbon between buttons, rosettes and buds. Stitch five to seven seed beads in groups at intervals along neckline. Stitch rice beads to rosette centers.

Nostalgic Nosegay

MATERIALS

5" white fabric square
7" green fabric circle
¾ yard of 3" white scalloped lace
1 yard of 1½" green wired ribbon
½-⅝ yard lengths of seven assorted silk ribbons
8" of 2" white organdy ribbon
3" Styrofoam ball

1" wired ribbon:
   ¾ yard of blue
   ¾ yard of peach
   ¾ yard of pink
   ¾ yard of purple
   ¾ yard of red
   ¾ yard of yellow
5" lightweight cardboard square

DIRECTIONS

1. Make small cone pattern on page 70. Cut one cone from cardboard and white fabric. Cut and discard half of Styrofoam ball.

2. Glue green circle over rounded area of ball, smoothing fullness around edges. Pulling snugly, wrap and glue edges to flat side of ball. Center cardboard cone on wrong side of white square. Pulling snugly, wrap and glue edges to back. Roll white cone with fabric side out. Overlap straight edges; glue.

3. Cut one 22" and one 4" length of scalloped lace. Wrap 4" length around cone, overlapping and gluing short ends. Glue top long edges inside cone. Fold 22" length in half, matching scallops and right sides facing. Stitch short ends; trim excess lace. Finger gather and glue straight edge to inside top edge of cone; fluff. Center green ball over cone opening and gathered lace, gluing flat side securely.

4. Make six rosettes from 27" lengths each of blue, peach, pink, purple, red and yellow 1" wired ribbon. Center and glue one rosette on green ball; glue remaining rosettes around center.

5. Fold green wired ribbon length in half with right sides facing. Stitch short ends. Stitch running thread on one long edge. Gather ribbon to fit around and under roses, gluing to ball. Glue gathered lace to flat side of green ball.

6. Handling the seven assorted ribbon lengths as one, fold in half. Knot ends together. Glue knot on seam at top of cone under gathered lace. Tie bow with white organdy ribbon; glue to cone covering knots.

Ribbons and Romance

MATERIALS

5" x 6" dusty rose print for back
5" x 6" of muslin
⅛" silk ribbon:
    1⅛ yards of beige
    1⅛ yards of brown
    1⅛ yards of dusty rose
    1⅛ yards of gray
    1⅛ yards of lavender
    1⅛ yards of pink
    1⅛ yards of purple
    1⅛ yards of tan
    ¾ yard of dark pink
¼" silk ribbon:
    5" of pink
    5" of tan

½ yard of ½" decorative trim
½ yard of ¼" cream picot trim
⅜ yard of ⅛" cream picot trim
½ yard of ⅜" cream lace
4" wide cream lace scrap or doily
5" small gold metallic braid
6" of 1" pink ribbon
Two brass charms
One antique jewelry piece
Eight assorted cream buttons
Six pearls
Polyester stuffing

DIRECTIONS

1. Make heart pattern on page 64. For woven ribbon heart, cut four 5" lengths and three 6½" lengths each of ⅛" beige, brown, dusty rose, gray, lavender, pink, purple and tan. Weave. Trace heart on right side of woven ribbons. Sew ⅜" cream lace with design toward center of heart.

2. With wrong sides facing, stitch woven piece to back on marking, leaving an opening. Repeat, stitching ⅛" outside first row. Trim ¹⁄₁₆" from outside row of stitches; press. Stuff. Stitch opening closed.

3. Glue ½" trim on back edge, mitering at point. Fold braid in half. Tie knot 1" from fold for hanger. Glue ends to heart front cleavage. Cover heart front with lace scrap as desired; glue edges. Weave pink ⅛" silk ribbon through ¼" picot trim. Align edges of woven trim to trim on back; glue. Loop and glue ⅛" picot trim to heart front as desired, anchoring trim with five pearls.

4. Stitch running thread on one long edge of 1" pink ribbon; gather to 1½". Glue to heart front cleavage. Glue jewelry to ribbon with charms and buttons on either side; see photo. Make a gathered circle with ¼" ribbons, gluing to heart front at point. Glue remaining pearl to center of gathered circle.

Fit for an Angel

MATERIALS

⅝ yard of 12-gauge covered wire
1½ yards of ⅝" pink satin ribbon
2 yards of ½" cream lace
½ yard of 5" flat white lace
6" of ½" white lace
⅛" picot trim:
    1 yard of cream
    1 yard of cream/gold metallic
⅛" ribbon silk ribbon:
    4½ yards of green
    4½ yards of light yellow
    2¼ yards of peach
    2¼ yards of pink
    2¼ yards of white

¼" silk ribbon:
    2¾ yards of pink
    ¾ yard of mauve
    ¾ yard of yellow
    ½ yard of white
¼" organdy ribbon:
    4¾ yards of cream
    4¾ yards of pink
⅞ yard of 2" pink organdy ribbon
1½" wired ribbon:
    1⅛" yards of pink
    ⅞ yard of pink plaid with picot edge
    ½ yard cream
    6" of green
Nine diamond-shaped cream buttons

DIRECTIONS

1. Bend wire to form a wreath. Tape ends, overlapping ½". Wrap and glue ⅝" pink satin ribbon to wreath. Sew a running thread on long edge of ½" cream lace; gather to 1 yard. Mark 3" at center back of wreath. Beginning and ending at each mark, wrap and glue lace to wreath at ½" intervals.

2. Sew a running thread on long edge of 5" white lace. Gather to 2"; center and glue gathering and short ends to center back of wreath. Glue ½" white lace over raw edges (see diagram).

3. Make ten ¼" layered rosettes with cream and pink organdy ribbons. Make ten ¼" silk ribbon rosettes: two pink, three mauve, three yellow and two white. Beginning and ending at each center back mark, cluster all flowers in pairs at 1" intervals. Center and glue buttons between each cluster.

4. Beginning and ending at center back marks, loosely spiral cream picot around wreath. Glue as needed. Repeat with cream/gold picot. Cut one 81" length each of ⅛" green and light yellow ribbon. Handling as one, tie nine small bows at 3" interval, leaving tails at beginning and end of ribbon length. Beginning at one center back mark, glue one set of tails to wreath. Loosely wrap ribbon once around

wreath, gluing first bow at first cluster. Repeat, attaching each bow to clusters.

5. Cut three 12" lengths of 2" pink organdy ribbon, tying two-looped bows without tails from each. Repeat with two 15" lengths of pink plaid ribbon, tying three-looped bows. Mark pink wired ribbon length with six 6" loops and a dot at loop centers. Knot loosely at dots; then make six-looped bow. Set aside.

6. Cut one 36" and three 15" lengths each from remaining ¼" cream and pink organdy and pink silk ribbon. Repeat from ⅛" light yellow, green, white, peach and pink silk ribbon. Handling 36" lengths as one, tie a bow with two 5" loops. Knot tails at varying lengths. Tie one bow without tails from each 15" length. Glue all bows to center back of wreath as desired; see photo.

7. Make two ribbon leaves from green wired ribbon. Glue leaves to center of bows. Make a gathered circle from an 18" length of cream wired ribbon. Fold gathered circle in half, gluing to top of bows. Fluff and shape ribbons.

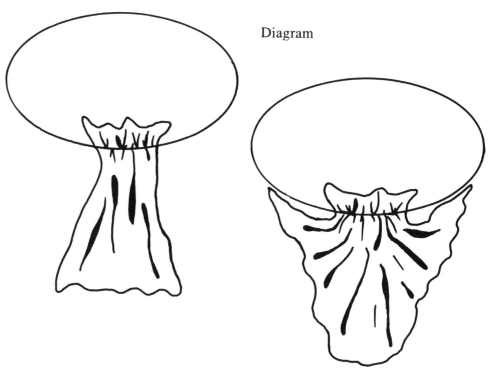

Diagram

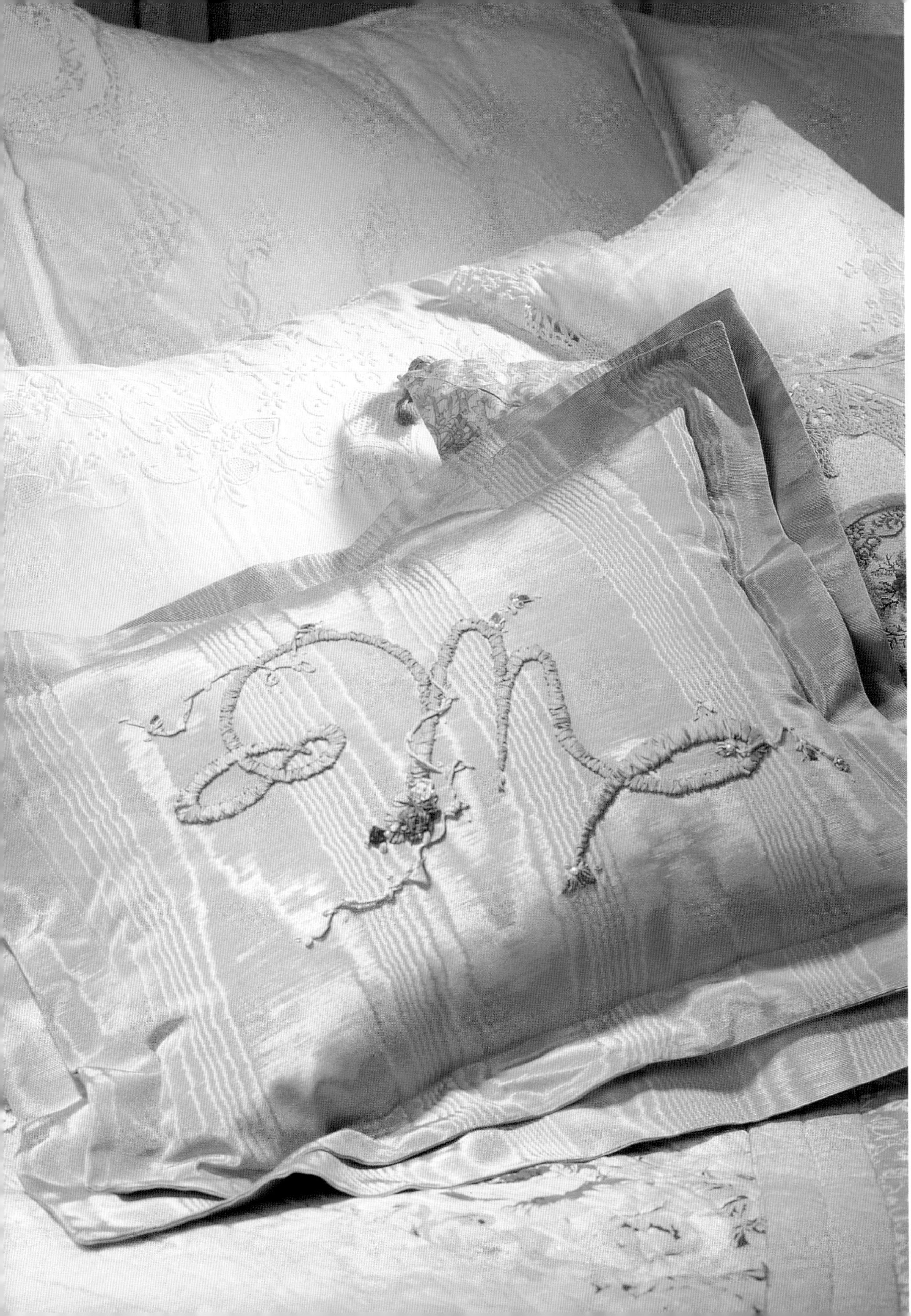

Personally Yours

MATERIALS

½ yard of purple moire
⅝ yard of tan moire
½ yard of muslin
⅛" silk ribbon:
    18 yards of purple
    1 yard of green
    ⅝ yard of burgundy
    ⅝ yard of dark purple
    ⅝ yard of peach
    ½ yard of teal

¼ yard of dark pink ¼" silk ribbon
Embroidery floss:
    Three pink shades
    One green shade
Small pearls
Embroidery hoop
Polyester stuffing

DIRECTIONS

All seams are ¼".

1. From purple, cut two 18" x 21" pillow fronts. From tan, cut two 21" x 24" pillow backs. From muslin, cut two 15" x 18" pieces.

2. Enlarge letter as desired. Center and transfer to one pillow front. Place fabric in hoop. Loosely satin stitch letter with ⅛" purple ribbon, keeping ribbon flat.

3. From ⅛" green ribbon, cut one 18" and two 9" lengths. Secure one end of 18" ribbon on wrong side of front, bringing up through letter center. Twist ribbon tightly. Tack remaining end to wrong side. Couch with teal ribbon to form vine. Repeat as desired.

4. Make three ⅛" rosettes: one each from burgundy, dark purple and peach ribbon. Make one ¼" rosette from dark pink ribbon. Tack to letter as desired. With remaining ⅛" ribbons, embroider buds around vines. With floss and ribbon, stitch bullion petals, buds and leaves around rosettes. Glue pearls as desired. Press on wrong side to smooth puckers.

5. Stitch pillow fronts with right sides facing, leaving an opening. Clip corners; turn. Slipstitch. Repeat for back. Stitch muslin pieces together, leaving an opening. Stuff firmly. Slipstitch closed.

6. With letter side up, mark 1½" in from front edges. Center front on back, stitch on marking, leaving one side open. Insert muslin pillow. Machine stitch closed.

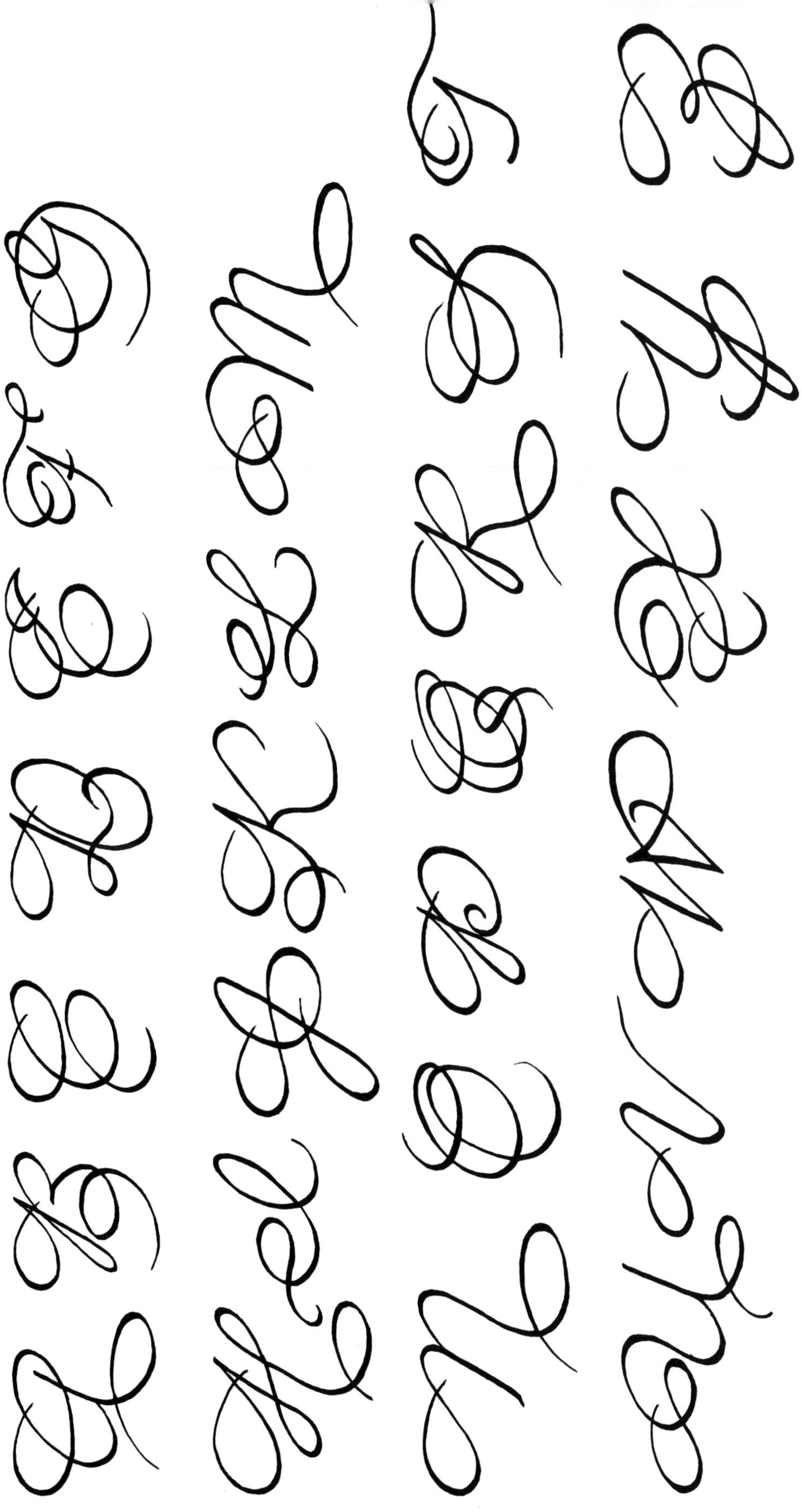

French Fancy

MATERIALS

⅜ yard print fabric
¼ yard brown fabric
18" x 7" coordinating print fabric
⅜ yard of fleece
1⅜ yards of ⅛" gold metallic braid
1 yard of ¼" gold metallic trim
¾ yard of 1" gold wired ribbon
1½ yards of ⅛" tan silk ribbon

1 yard of ¼" picot trim
½ yard of ³⁄₁₆" brown velvet ribbon
Eleven assorted fabric scraps
One large blue iridescent button
Fusible webbing
1" x 6" dowel
24" x 36" heavyweight cardboard piece
24" x 36" lightweight cardboard piece

DIRECTIONS

1 Make patterns. Cut cardboard, fabric and fleece (F), according to chart. Score lightweight cardboard pieces as indicated (see Diagram A on page 91).

	HEAVY WT. CARDBOARD	LIGHT WT. CARDBOARD	PRINT	BROWN	COORDI-NATING	F
LID	2		adding ½"	adding ½"		2
LID SIDE		1	22⅜" x 3"			
TRAY	2				adding ½"	
TRAY SIDE		1			16¾" x 3"	
INSERT	1			adding ½"		1
INSERT SIDE		1		23½" x 3½"		1
BASE	1		adding ½"			
BOX SIDE		1	24⅛" x 7½"			

2. Glue and layer fleece pieces to one LID. Center cardboard/fleece LID, fleece-side down, on wrong side of print LID. Pulling snugly, wrap and glue edges to wrong side. Repeat with INSERT, gluing fleece on unscored INSERT SIDE.

3. Center and laminate remaining LID, TRAYs, and BASE. Laminate BOX SIDE on scored side, centering cardboard on wrong side of print BOX SIDE horizontally, aligning one long edge and leaving 3" on opposite long edge. Pulling snugly, wrap and glue edges to wrong side, clipping corners.

4. Laminate LID SIDE, centering cardboard horizontally, leaving ½" allowance on one long edge and 2½" on opposite long edge. Pulling snugly, wrap and glue one short end to cardboard. Then, glue 2½" edge, aligning raw edges. Set aside. Repeat with TRAY SIDE. Let side pieces dry slightly.

5. To curve, lay BOX SIDE right-side down. Fold on scores. Roll dowel across folds, making distinct corners. Unfold, turning right-side up. Place dowel 1½" in front of first corner, rolling cardboard tightly around dowel to corner. Place dowel just behind first corner, rolling cardboard 1½". Place dowel 1½" in front of second corner, rolling cardboard to corner. Place dowel just behind second corner, rolling cardboard 2½". Place dowel 2½" in front of third corner, rolling cardboard to corner. Place dowel just behind third corner, rolling cardboard 1½". Place dowel 1½" in front of fourth corner, rolling to corner. Place dowel just behind fourth corner, rolling cardboard 1½".

6. Turn piece wrong-side up. At ends and centers between each corner, roll cardboard, forming a series of "S" curves. Repeat with LID SIDE. Repeat for TRAY SIDE, beginning at second corner and leaving 5½" space in front of first corner uncurved. Repeat for INSERT SIDE, beginning with padded side up.

7. Place LID SIDE (seam allowance down) around coordinating print LID (right side up), aligning corners (see Diagram B). Beginning at first corner, glue outer edges of LID to inner edge of LID SIDE. Continue gluing small sections at a time. Complete, overlapping short ends, gluing finished end on top. Glue allowance to wrong side of LID. Center and glue wrong sides of LIDs together. Repeat to complete TRAY and INSERT.

Diagram B

8. Repeat Step 7, gluing BOX SIDE around INSERT. Then, glue BASE to wrong side of INSERT.

9. Cut two 24" lengths of gold metallic braid and one 24" length of gold metallic trim, set remaining trim aside. Glue braid along outside edges of LID seam. Repeat on box bottom along lip of BASE. Glue 1" wired ribbon above braid. Glue gold trim to top edge of wired ribbon.

10. Make a yo-yo from one fabric scrap. Fuse webbing to remaining scraps, according to manufacturer's instructions. Cut eight diamonds and two squares from scraps. Center and fuse shapes on LID (pattern on LID). Cut seven 2" lengths of brown ribbon. Glue over raw adjacent edges of diamonds. With remaining metallic trim, cut two 3½" lengths. Glue to outer edges of squares. Weave ⅛" tan ribbon through picot trim. Glue to outer edges of diamonds. Stitch button to center of design, forming an indent. Center and glue yo-yo inside LID.

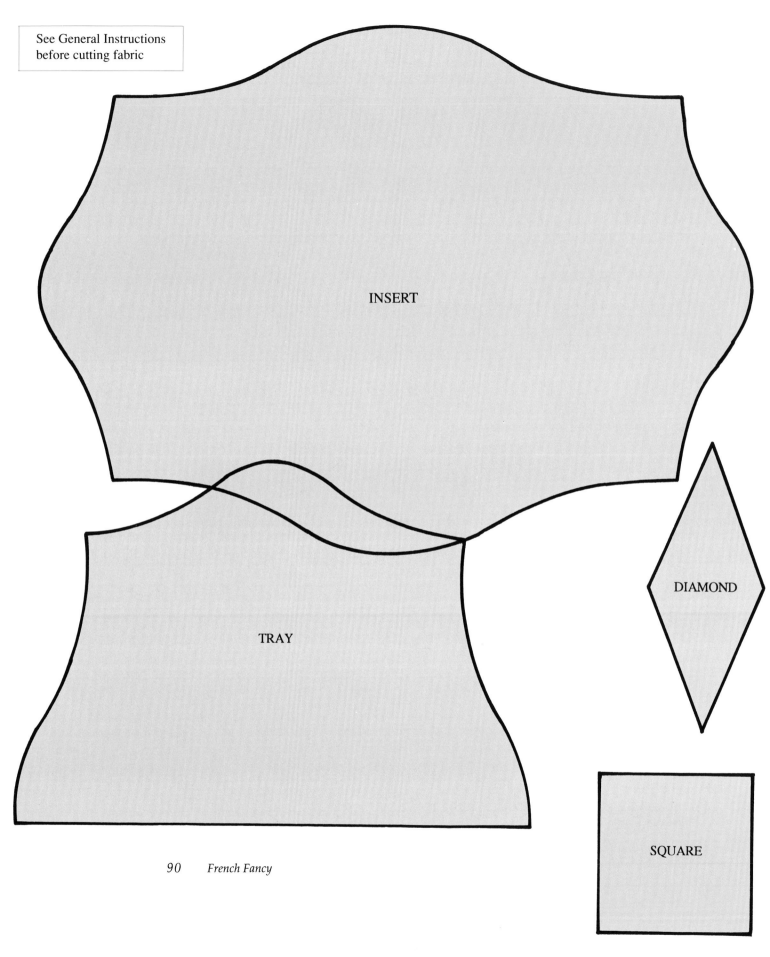

See General Instructions
before cutting fabric

INSERT

DIAMOND

TRAY

SQUARE

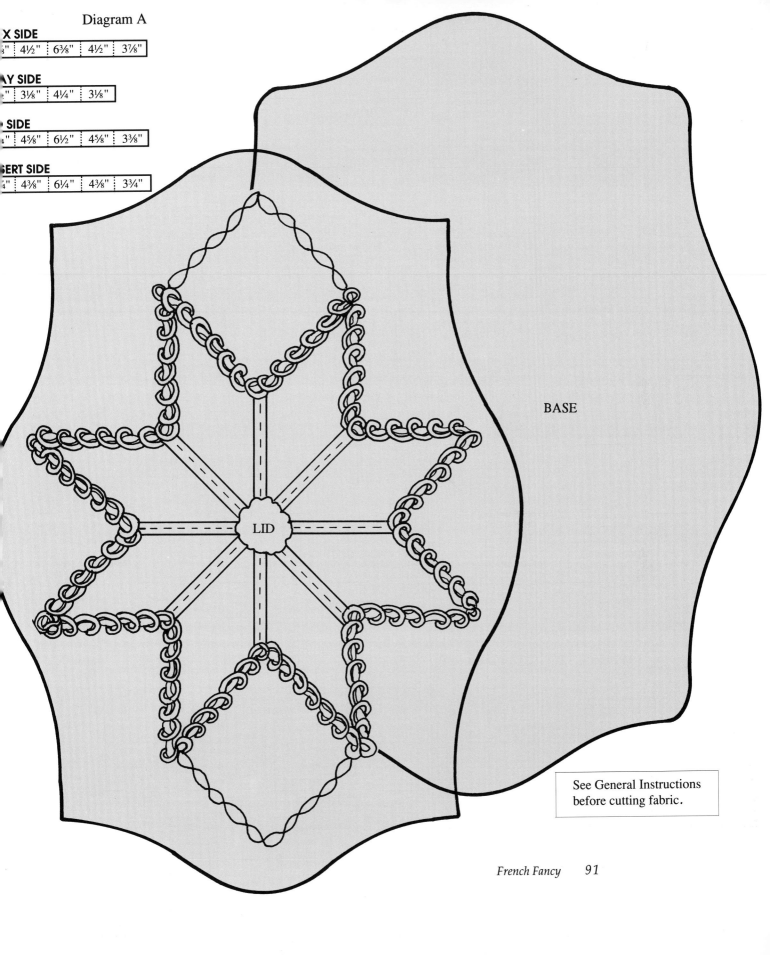

X SIDE

| | 4½" | 6⅜" | 4½" | 3⅞" |

AY SIDE

| | 3⅛" | 4¼" | 3⅛" |

SIDE

| | 4⅝" | 6½" | 4⅝" | 3⅜" |

SERT SIDE

| | 4⅜" | 6¼" | 4⅜" | 3¾" |

BASE

LID

See General Instructions
before cutting fabric.

Antique Embellished Heart

MATERIALS

15" x 16" green velvet
7½" x 8" fleece piece
7½" x 8" cream lace fabric
¼ yard of rose trim
½ yard of ⅜" cream lace trim
13" of ⅝" cream lace trim
½ yard of 3" cream scalloped lace
¼ yard of ½" purple wired ribbon
¼" silk ribbon:
   ¾ yard of cream
   ¼ yard of green
   ¼ yard of rust
   ¼ yard of tan

1" wired ribbon:
   1⅝ yards of orange metallic
   1 yard of green
⅛" silk ribbon:
   ¾ yard of blue
   ¾ yard of light green
   ¾ yard of tan
   1½ yards of dark green
   1½ yards of peach
   1½ yards of rust
Four fancy buttons
Eight assorted brass charms
70 assorted pearls, seed beads, sequins
Purchased, old-fashioned greeting card
15" x 7" lightweight cardboard piece

DIRECTIONS

1. Make patterns. Cut two large hearts each from cardboard and green fabric and one large heart each from fleece and lace. Trace small heart on card as desired; cut out.

2. For front, glue fleece to one cardboard heart. Clip edges of green hearts. Center and glue cardboard/fleece heart, fleece side down, on wrong side of green heart. Pulling snugly, wrap and glue fabric edge to wrong side. Repeat, layering lace heart over green heart. For back, glue remaining cardboard heart to green heart.

3. Glue rose trim to front of card-heart edge. Sew running stitch on long straight edge of ⅜" cream trim. Gather and glue to back of card-heart edge. Center and glue card heart to heart front.

4. For ruched ribbon, mark 1" orange ribbon at 3" intervals, stitch and gather tightly. To overlap scallops, glue gathered edges to wrong side of heart-front edge, turning and gluing every other scallop (see diagram).

5. For hanger, cut 9" of 1" green wired ribbon; set remaining length aside. Fold in an inverted "V". Center and glue ends to wrong side of heart front at top.

6. To embellish hanger, make one gathered circle from 13" of 1" green wired ribbon. Repeat with ⅝" cream trim. Center and glue green gathered circle to hanger fold. Glue cream gathered circle to green circle. Make one violet from ½" purple wired ribbon. Glue to cream circle. Glue one pearl to center of violet .

7. Fold remaining length of green wired ribbon in an inverted "V", with one tail longer. Clip tails in an inverted "V"; see photo. Glue fold to wrong side of heart front at point. Glue one charm to each tail.

8. To embellish heart front, make three ¼" layered rosettes: one with cream/green, one with cream/rust and one with cream/tan ribbon. Attach rosettes to top edge of heart front. Cut 27" lengths each of ⅛" dark green, peach and rust ribbon. Handling as one, tie small bow. Glue to front cleavage. Cascade tails. Glue one button to center of bow. Attach remaining charms, buttons, pearls, seed beads and sequins to front as desired.

9. Beginning and ending 3" from cleavage, glue 3" scalloped lace to wrong side of front edge. Handling remaining ⅛" lengths as one, tie small bow. Glue to scalloped lace at point of heart front. Knot tails. Divide tails; wrap loosely to back of green wired tails; knot. Center and glue wrong sides of heart front and back together.

Diagram

SMALL HEART

See General Instructions
before cutting fabric.

LARGE   HEART

See General Instructions
before cutting fabric.

Legacy of Lace

MATERIALS

⅜ yard of tapestry
⅜ yard of blue moire
⅜ yard of blue lining
Assorted lace scraps
Eighteen 2½" circles from assorted fabrics
1¼ yards of ½" white gathered lace
⅝ yard of 1½" pink silk ribbon
⅛" silk ribbon:
    1⅜ yards of pink
    ⅝ yard of blue
    ⅝ yard of gray
    ⅝ yard of purple
    10" of lavender
    10" of peach
    10" of white
    10" of yellow

¼" silk ribbon:
    ¼ yard of beige
    ¼ yard of pink
    ¼ yard of yellow
¼ yard of ⅛" cream picot trim
⅛" yard of ¼" rose satin picot ribbon
    for hanger
Silk embroidery floss:
    three pink shades
    two green shades
¼ yard of ½" decorative trim
Eleven small flat cream buttons
1½" rhinestone strand
100-150 assorted bugle beads, pearls,
    seed beads

DIRECTIONS
All seams are ¼".

1. Make pattern. Mark pattern for stocking front on blue moire; do not cut out. From tapestry, cut one stocking back. From lining, cut one stocking front and one back. Crazy quilt lace to right side of stocking front; cut out.

2. Embroider a stitched ribbon rose at center of toe. To make stitched ribbon rose use 4" of ⅛" pink ribbon. Sew small stitches, circling inward and stitching closely so fabric does not show through (see Diagram A). Finish center with French knot. Cut one 17" length of ⅛" blue ribbon. Tie small bow. Attach to rose on toe. Cascade tails. Scatter bullion petals, leaves and seed beads as desired.

3. Stitch eight buttons at 1" intervals around heel of stocking front 1" from edge. Cut one 17" length of ⅛" pink ribbon. Tie small bow. Attach to center button on heel. Cascade tails. Attach 2-3 seed beads between cascading.

4. Make three ¼" rosettes: one each from beige, pink and yellow ribbon. Make twelve ⅛" rosettes: one each from pink, blue, purple and gray; two each from

lavender, peach, white, and yellow ribbon. Stitch rosettes and rhinestone strand on stocking front in a 2¼" circle where desired. Cut one 17" length each of ⅛" gray and purple ribbon. Handling as one, tie small bow. Attach at center bottom of circle. Cascade tails in figure "8s" (see Diagram B). Bead wreath and intersections as desired. With remaining ⅛" pink ribbon, embroider buds at random around wreath.

5. With right sides facing and raw edges aligned, stitch stocking front to back, leaving top open. Clip curves. Turn. Repeat for stocking lining, leaving large opening in side seam above heel. Do not turn. With right sides facing, slide lining over stocking, matching side seams. With raw edges aligned, stitch lining to stocking on top edge. Turn stocking through heel opening in lining. Slipstitch opening closed. Tuck lining inside stocking.

6. Beginning and ending 1½" from side seam on top edge of stocking front, slipstitch gathered lace around seam. Make thirteen fabric yo-yos and five fabric leaves. Stitch across top edge of stocking front, covering raw ends of lace. Stitch beads and buttons at random. Loop picot trim around top edge, tacking as needed. Fold hanger in half; stitch ends to inside top edge of stocking at heel side.

7. Knife pleat 1½" pink ribbon. Sew decorative trim over stitches on back of pleating. Slipstitch to inside top edge of stocking front.

Diagram A   Diagram B

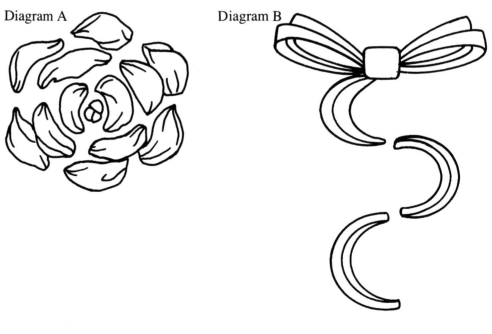

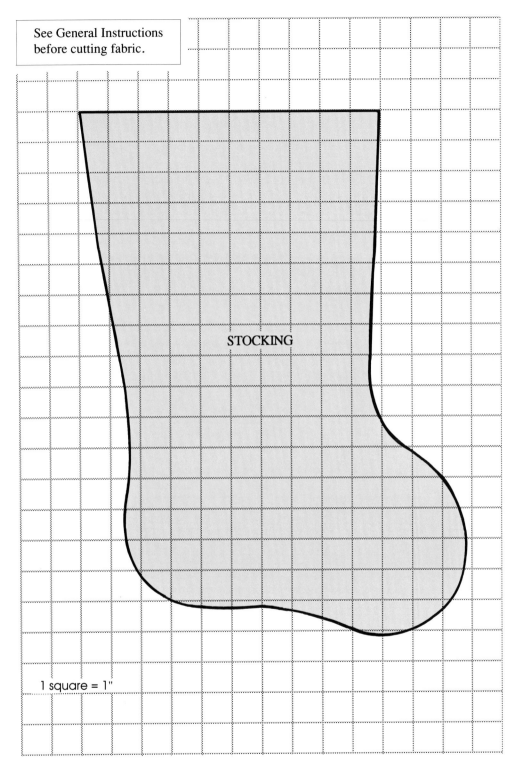

See General Instructions
before cutting fabric.

STOCKING

1 square = 1"

Lavish Lace Vest

MATERIALS

Purchased vest pattern with required
    fabrics and notions
Assorted lace and doily scraps for
    crazy quilting
⅛" silk ribbon:
    3⅜ yards of blue
    3¼ yards of pink
    2⅜ yards of lavender
    1¾ yards of light green
    1¾ yards of white
    1 yard of yellow
    1 yard of gray
    ¾ yard of peach
    ¾ yard of dusty rose
    ½ yard of green
    ⅜ yard of purple
¼" silk ribbon:
    ¼ yard of purple
    ¼ yard of lavender
    ¼ yard of yellow

½" silk ribbon:
    ⅜ yard of pink
    ⅜ yard of white
¾ yard of 1" white wired ribbon
¼ yard of ½" pink wired ribbon
½ yard of ⅛" cream/gold metallic picot trim
¼ yard of ¼" white lace
Silk embroidery floss:
    Three pink shades
    Two green shades
3½" muslin square
Nine ⅜" flat cream buttons
Seven ¼" cream buttons
Five ⅝" fancy buttons for closure
Five assorted brass heart charms
Eight assorted brass charms
100-150 assorted pearls, seed beads, sequins
3" fusible webbing square

DIRECTIONS

All seams are ¼".

1. Make heart pattern on page 103. Cut vest front, back and lining, according to purchased pattern. Crazy-quilt lace to right side of vest fronts.

2. For woven ribbon heart, cut 27" lengths each of ⅛" blue, pink, lavender, light green, yellow and gray ribbons. Cut each length into six 4½" strips. Weave. Trace and topstitch heart on bias on right side of woven ribbons. Repeat, stitching ¹⁄₁₆" outside first row. Fuse webbing to back, according to manufacturer's instructions. Cut woven heart ¹⁄₁₆" outside stitching. Fuse heart to vest front as desired; stitch edges. With design toward center, sew ¼" lace on heart edge covering stitches.

3. Make sixteen ⅛" rosettes: two each of blue, lavender, yellow, purple, gray, three each of peach and dusty rose ribbon. Make one ¼" layered rosette with purple/lavender ribbons and one ¼" rosette from yellow ribbon. Make five ⅛" pencil daisies: one each from blue, pink, white, peach and dusty rose ribbon.

4. Tack ⅛" rosettes on woven heart edge; set one aside. With ⅛" light green ribbon, stitch leaves around rosettes. Cut 18" lengths each of ⅛" pink, lavender and light green ribbon. Handling as one, tie small bow. Tack to woven heart top. Cascade tails. Tack beads and sequins to tails and remaining rosette to bow center.

5. For ruched ribbon, layer 12¼" lengths each of ½" white and pink ribbon. Mark at 1¾" intervals, stitch and gather. Tack bottom layer to vest; anchor centers with embroidered silk ribbon leaves. Attach one fancy button and ⅛" rosette as desired. Cut 18" lengths each of ⅛" pink and blue silk ribbon. Handling as one, tie small bow. Tack to rosette. Cascade tails.

6. Loop picot trim as desired. Embroider rosettes, buds and leaves with remaining ⅛" silk ribbon as desired. Embroider bullion petals and leaves with floss.

7. String heart charms as desired on left vest front. Loosely stitch ⅛" lavender and blue ribbon around charms. Attach five to seven seed beads between stitches. Cut one 13" length of ⅛" pink ribbon. Tie small bow; attach to charms. Cascade tails. Tack beads and sequins to tails. Tack yellow ¼" rosette to bow center. Repeat on right vest front with remaining charms. Loosely stitch ⅛" pink ribbon around charms. Cut one 22" length each of ⅛" blue and lavender ribbon. Handling as one, tie small bow; attach to charms. Cascade tails. Tack beads and sequins to tails and pencil daisys as desired.

8. On right vest front, stitch nine flat buttons at 1" intervals 1⅛" from neck edge. With ⅛" pink ribbon, stitch buds at each button. Stitch bullion petals around buds with floss. Scatter lazy daisy leaves, French knots, seed beads and sequins around roses. Repeat on left vest front as desired with ¼" buttons; omit seed beads.

9. For a pointed petal flower, cut eleven 2¼" lengths of 1" wired ribbon for petals. Fold top corners of one petal toward center, forming triangle. Fold bottom corners to back overlapping ¼" at center (see diagram). Sew running thread on straight edge; gather. Repeat for remaining petals. With petal backs up and gathers toward center, form a ¾" circle as desired on vest. Tack petals, overlapping slightly. Make a gathered circle from 9" of ⅜" pink wired ribbon. Tack gathered circle to pointed petal flower center. Attach one fancy button to center. Cut one 22" length each of ⅛" pink, blue and white ribbon. Handling as one, tie small bow; attach to one petal. Cascade tails. Tack beads and sequins to tails.

10. Assemble vest according to instructions. Topstitch outer seams. Stitch buttonholes on vest front; cut. Whipstitch buttonholes with ⅛" white silk ribbon. Embroider buds and leaves around holes with ⅛" silk ribbon. Stitch remaining fancy buttons on opposite vest front.

HEART
for vest

BOX BOTTOM

Diagram

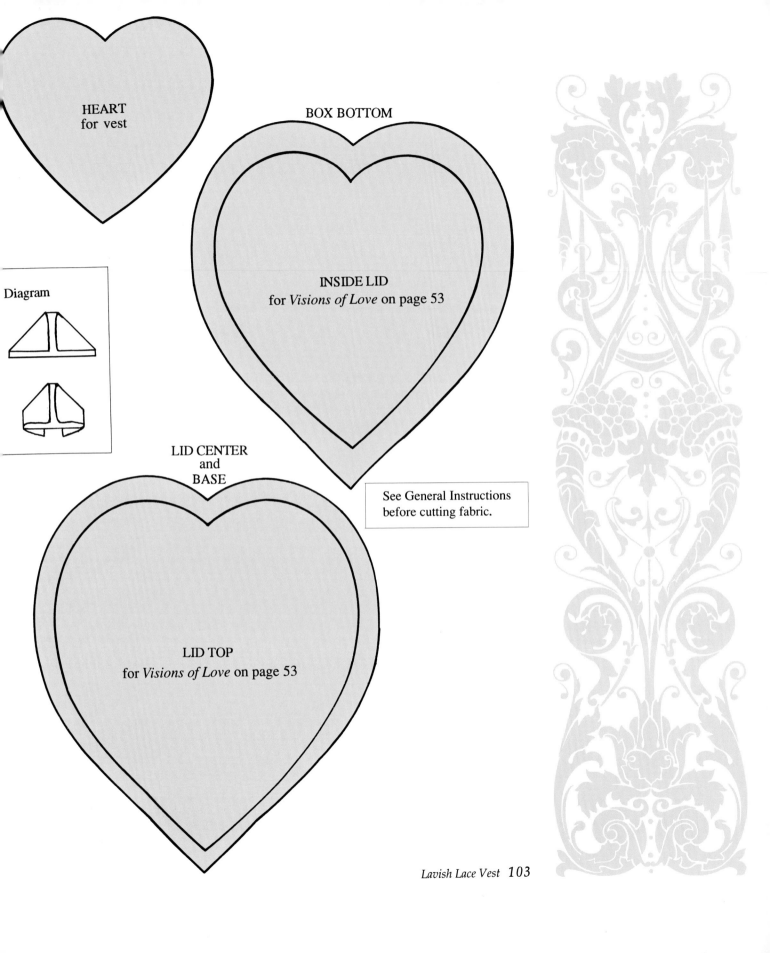

INSIDE LID
for *Visions of Love* on page 53

LID CENTER
and
BASE

See General Instructions
before cutting fabric.

LID TOP
for *Visions of Love* on page 53

Charles Dickens
A Christmas Carol
Illustrated by Brian Robert Thomas

METRIC EQUIVALENCY CHART

MM-Millimetres   CM-Centimetres

INCHES TO MILLIMETRES AND CENTIMETRES

INCHES	MM	CM	INCHES	CM	INCHES	CM
⅛	3	0.3	9	22.9	30	76.2
¼	6	0.6	10	25.4	31	78.7
⅜	10	1.0	11	27.9	32	81.3
½	13	1.3	12	30.5	33	83.8
⅝	16	1.6	13	33.0	34	86.4
¾	19	1.9	14	35.6	35	88.9
⅞	22	2.2	15	38.1	36	91.4
1	25	2.5	16	40.6	37	94.0
1¼	32	3.2	17	43.2	38	96.5
1½	38	3.8	18	45.7	39	99.1
1¾	44	4.4	19	48.3	40	101.6
2	51	5.1	20	50.8	41	104.1
2½	64	6.4	21	53.3	42	106.7
3	76	7.6	22	55.9	43	109.2
3½	89	8.9	23	58.4	44	111.8
4	102	10.2	24	61.0	45	114.3
4½	114	11.4	25	63.5	46	116.8
5	127	12.7	26	66.0	47	119.4
6	152	15.2	27	68.6	48	121.9
7	178	17.8	28	71.1	49	124.5
8	203	20.3	29	73.7	50	127.0

YARDS TO METRES

YARDS	METRES	YARDS	METRES	YARDS	METRES	YARDS	METRES	YARDS	METRES
⅛	0.11	2⅛	1.94	4⅛	3.77	6⅛	5.60	8⅛	7.43
¼	0.23	2¼	2.06	4¼	3.89	6¼	5.72	8¼	7.54
⅜	0.34	2⅜	2.17	4⅜	4.00	6⅜	5.83	8⅜	7.66
½	0.46	2½	2.29	4½	4.11	6½	5.94	8½	7.77
⅝	0.57	2⅝	2.40	4⅝	4.23	6⅝	6.06	8⅝	7.89
¾	0.69	2¾	2.51	4¾	4.34	6¾	6.17	8¾	8.00
⅞	0.80	2⅞	2.63	4⅞	4.46	6⅞	6.29	8⅞	8.12
1	0.91	3	2.74	5	4.57	7	6.40	9	8.23
1⅛	1.03	3⅛	2.86	5⅛	4.69	7⅛	6.52	9⅛	8.34
1¼	1.14	3¼	2.97	5¼	4.80	7¼	6.63	9¼	8.46
1⅜	1.26	3⅜	3.09	5⅜	4.91	7⅜	6.74	9⅜	8.57
1½	1.37	3½	3.20	5½	5.03	7½	6.86	9½	8.69
1⅝	1.49	3⅝	3.31	5⅝	5.14	7⅝	6.97	9⅝	8.80
1¾	1.60	3¾	3.43	5¾	5.26	7¾	7.09	9¾	8.92
1⅞	1.71	3⅞	3.54	5⅞	5.37	7⅞	7.20	9⅞	9.03
2	1.83	4	3.66	6	5.49	8	7.32	10	9.14

Index